SHAKESPEARE

# HAMLET
# IN EVERYDAY
# ENGLISH

COLES EDITORIAL BOARD

Bound to stay open

**Publisher's Note**

Otabind (Ota-bind). This book has been bound using the patented Otabind process. You can open this book at any page, gently run your finger down the spine, and the pages will lie flat.

## ABOUT COLES NOTES

COLES NOTES have been an indispensible aid to students on five continents since 1948.

COLES NOTES are available for a wide range of individual literary works. Clear, concise explanations and insights are provided along with interesting interpretations and evaluations.

Proper use of COLES NOTES will allow the student to pay greater attention to lectures and spend less time taking notes. This will result in a broader understanding of the work being studied and will free the student for increased participation in discussions.

COLES NOTES are an invaluable aid for review and exam preparation as well as an invitation to explore different interpretive paths.

COLES NOTES are written by experts in their fields. It should be noted that any literary judgement expressed herein is just that – the judgement of one school of thought. Interpretations that diverge from, or totally disagree with any criticism may be equally valid.

COLES NOTES are designed to supplement the text and are not intended as a substitute for reading the text itself. Use of the NOTES will serve not only to clarify the work being studied, but should enhance the readers enjoyment of the topic.

**ISBN 0-7740-3748-2**

© COPYRIGHT 1998 AND PUBLISHED BY
**COLES PUBLISHING COMPANY**
TORONTO - CANADA
PRINTED IN CANADA

Manufactured by Webcom Limited
Cover finish: Webcom's Exclusive **DURACOAT**

# CHARACTERS IN THE PLAY

**Claudius:** King of Denmark
**Hamlet:** Son of the former king and Claudius' nephew
**Horatio:** Friend of Hamlet
**Polonius:** Lord Chamberlain
**Laertes:** Polonius' son
**Voltimand**
**Cornelius**
**Rosencrantz** } Courtiers
**Guildenstern**
**Osric**
**Marcellus** } Officers
**Bernardo**
**Francisco:** A soldier
**Reynaldo:** Servant of Polonius
**A Captain**
**Ambassadors**
**Ghost of Hamlet's father**
**Fortinbras:** Prince of Norway
**Two Clowns:** Gravediggers
**Gertrude:** Queen of Denmark and Hamlet's mother
**Ophelia:** Polonius' daughter
**Lords, Ladies, Officers, Soldiers, Players, Sailors, Messengers and Attendants**

*[Setting: Elsinore.]*

## ACT I · SCENE 1

*[Elsinore. A platform before the castle.]*
*[Francisco at his post. Enter Bernardo.]*

**Bernardo:** Is anyone there?

**Francisco:** Reply to me first, sir. Halt, and give the word.

**Bernardo:** Long live the king!

**Francisco:** Not Bernardo, surely?

**Bernardo:** The same.

**Francisco:** You are punctual tonight, are you not?

**Bernardo:** It has just tolled midnight. Go to your rest, Francisco.

**Francisco:** I am thankful, indeed, that my duty is ended. The air is piercingly keen, and my spirit is weary.

**Bernardo:** Have you anything to report?

**Francisco:** I have not noticed the slightest movement of a living creature.

**Bernardo:** Good night, then. Should you happen to encounter Horatio and Marcellus, my companions in duty, tell them to be speedy.

**Francisco:** Here they are now, I fancy. Hold, there! Say who you are!

*[Enter Horatio and Marcellus.]*

**Horatio:** True sons of Denmark.

**Marcellus:** And loyal subjects of her king.

**Francisco:** Good night, sirs.

**Marcellus:** O, good-bye, my trusty fellow. Whom have you left in your place?

**Francisco:** Bernardo is there now. Good night, sirs.

*[Exit.]*

**Marcellus:** Are you there, Bernardo?

**Bernardo:** Yes. What, is that Horatio?

**Horatio:** Something like him.

**Bernardo:** I am pleased indeed to greet you both.

**Horatio:** Well, have you seen this phantom of yours, since you came on duty?

**Bernardo:** Not as yet.

**Marcellus:** Horatio absolutely refuses to believe that this awe-inspiring sight that we have twice seen has any existence, except in our own fancies. So I have brought him along to keep watch with us tonight, that, if this apparition should appear again, he may confirm the testimony of our own

1

eyesight and, being a scholar, address it.

**Horatio:** Nonsense, I shall see nothing.

**Bernardo:** Be seated a moment, while we give yet another account of our experiences during the last two nights, which you steadfastly refuse to believe.

**Horatio:** Well, we will sit down then, and hear Bernardo tell the story this time.

**Bernardo:** But yesternight, when that very star that is shining yonder to the west of the Pole occupied its present position in the heavens, and just as the clock was striking one, Marcellus and I—

[*Enter ghost.*]

**Marcellus:** Hush, say no more; lo, the spirit itself is here.

**Bernardo:** Just as before, in the likeness of the dead king.

**Marcellus:** You can utter an exorcism; address it, Horatio.

**Bernardo:** Is it not the image of his majesty? Notice it, Horatio!

**Horatio:** It is so like him that my mind is torn with terror and amazement.

**Bernardo:** It wishes to be questioned.

**Marcellus:** Ask what it desires, Horatio.

**Horatio:** What is thy nature, O form, that invadest this hour of the night, assuming without right, the goodly and martial appearance in which Denmark's buried king used to walk? In heaven's name, I bid thee, answer me.

**Marcellus:** You have displeased it.

**Bernardo:** Look how majestically it moves away!

**Horatio:** Remain! and answer me! I bid thee, answer me!

[*Exit ghost.*]

**Marcellus:** It has departed without a word.

**Bernardo:** Well, Horatio, your ashen face betrays your agitation. What is your opinion now? Is it merely a creation of our fancy?

**Horatio:** Upon my word, I could not have believed it unless I had really and truly witnessed it with my own eyes.

**Marcellus:** Is it not the image of our late monarch?

**Horatio:** The resemblance could not possibly be closer. Clad in that selfsame suit of mail, he fought his famous duel with Norway's aspiring king. Thus did he scowl, when, during a heated conference with the Poles held on the frozen river, he overthrew them, sitting in their sleds. I cannot understand it.

2

**Marcellus:** On two previous occasions during our guard, has he stalked past us, in the same warlike manner and at precisely the same ghostly hour.

**Horatio:** What special line of thought to follow, I do not know but, speaking generally, I should say that this appearance predicts some startling disturbance in the affairs of our nation.

**Marcellus:** That reminds me. Take your seats again, and perhaps someone may be able to inform me the reason for the close and careful guard that is being kept continuously at present, throughout the whole of the country; for the number of brass cannons turned out every day by the arsenals and the quantities of warlike material purchased in foreign markets; why, too, so many shipwrights are compelled to work the whole week through and lose thereby their usual sabbath rest. What danger threatens us that these hasty preparations cause men to work night as well as day. Who can tell me, I wonder?

**Horatio:** I think I can tell the reason, or at least the rumored reason. As you are probably aware, Fortinbras, of Norway, incited by a haughty desire to excel, challenged our late king, whose spirit we have just now seen, to a personal encounter. In this encounter, our heroic monarch (for so, of course, we all considered him) slew Fortinbras, and by a duly signed agreement, drawn up strictly in accordance with the formalities of the court of chivalry, the latter surrendered to the vanquisher, as a result of his defeat, the whole of the lands in his possession. On the other hand, Hamlet had pledged an equivalent piece of territory, to be given to Fortinbras in the event of his being the conqueror, just as, by the claims of the articles drawn up, his lands became the property of our sovereign.

Well, gentlemen, Fortinbras' son, full of the rashness and inexperience of youth, has raked indiscriminately together from all parts of Norway a number of unruly desperadoes, willing, for no pay but their keep, to take part in any enterprise that will afford an outlet for their courage, and the object of this enterprise is undoubtedly to compel us by force to restore to him the above-mentioned lands that his father so justly lost. This, at any rate, appears to me to be the opinion of our rulers, and explains

3

our preparations for war, the strict lookout that is being kept and the bustle and turmoil that is disturbing the country.

**Bernardo:** What you say is no doubt true. Indeed, it is quite in accordance with this, that this ill-omened visitor who has thus disturbed our vigil should appear in battle array, and assume the likeness of the king who has been, and is, the cause of all these troubles.

**Horatio:** It is a mere nothing, however, compared with the greater trouble it implies. When Rome was at the height of her glory, just before the downfall of the great Julius, the tombs lay open, and their occupants enveloped in shrouds went squealing and gabbling through the streets of the city. Comets with fiery tails were seen in the sky bringing blood-red dews in their train; spots covered the face of the sun, and the watery moon, governor of the mighty deep, was almost as totally darkened as she will appear on God's high judgment day. And similar forewarnings of terrible happenings, like forerunners constantly going before the fates and preludes of dreadful things to come, have earth and sky conspired to grant unto our country and her people.

*[Re-enter ghost.]*

But hush, look! See, the figure is here once more. I'll step over its pathway regardless of the consequences. Hold, phantom form! And if it be at all within thy power, say something: if any benevolent action requires doing, which may bring rest to thee and a blessing on myself, tell me of it; if some great danger threatens our land from which she may escape by thy foreknowledge, O, let me hear it! Or if there be some secret store of ill-gotten wealth hidden away beneath the solid ground, which, it is said, often prevents the dead from resting in their graves, reveal its situation; stop, and reveal it! *[Cock crows.]* Don't let it go, Marcellus.

**Marcellus:** Must I use my weapon on it?

**Horatio:** Yes, if nothing else will stop it.

**Bernardo:** It's near me.

**Horatio:** It's near me.

**Marcellus:** It's vanished altogether! *[Exit ghost.]* We do a great injustice to this figure, so kingly in its bearing, by even pretending to restrain it by force, because, being as difficult

4

to wound as the atmosphere itself, our blows are mere fruitless labor, the outcome of ill will.

**Bernardo:** It would have spoken then, if that bird had not crowed.

**Horatio:** And that startled it as if it were a criminal summoned to his doom. The cock, I have been told, sounds the clarion which ushers in the dawn, and when he rears his head aloft and utters his piercing call, the guardian deity of the daytime awakens. At this signal all wandering spirits, wherever they may chance to stray, in flood or flame, in land or sky, hasten to their own proper limits. And the present instance tends to strengthen the truth of this statement.

**Marcellus:** It disappeared when the cock crowed. It is commonly said that when the time approaches in which we commemorate the birth of our Lord, this bird crows from dusk to dawn. Then, we are told, all spirits are restrained from wandering, the nights cease to infect, and the charms of fairies and witches are useless, so holy and so blessed is that time.

**Horatio:** I, too, am acquainted with this saying, and think there is some truth in it. But, see! The morn is breaking. Look how it reddens the sky beyond yon dewy hill to the east! Let us bring our guard to an end and, as I recommend, give an account of our experiences to Prince Hamlet, for I am firmly convinced that though it was so silent to us, the apparition will converse with him. Is it not your opinion that considerations alike of love and duty urge us to adopt this course?

**Marcellus:** Yes, I am strongly in favor of so doing, and can tell you where we shall have the best chance of finding him.

[*Exit.*]

## ACT I · SCENE 2

[*A room in the castle.*]
[*Enter the king, queen, Hamlet, Polonius, Laertes, Voltimand, Cornelius, lords and attendants.*]

**King:** Although we still cherish a tender recollection of the late king, our beloved brother, and although, as was right and proper, we were sorrow-stricken at his death, and our whole realm was plunged into general mourning, still prudence has to such an extent overcome this natural inclination, that our grief for him is now wisely tempered with some regard for our own welfare. Thus then, with a happiness somewhat marred by grief, with cheerful eyes bedimmed with tears, mingling the burial hymn with the marriage song, and endeavoring to preserve a just balance between joy and grief, we have taken our former sister to be our consort, the joint possessor with us of this martial kingdom. And, in this matter, we have not acted without the assent of your riper judgments, for you have spontaneously approved of all we have done, and we thank you for it.

Now we come to something of which you are already aware. Fortinbras' son, having a contemptuous opinion of our abilities, or supposing that, owing to the death of our much lamented predecessor, the affairs of our country are completely disorganized, has allied himself to this imaginary advantage, and continues to annoy us with communications, calling upon us to restore to him the territory forfeited by his parent to our heroic brother in full accordance with the terms of their agreement. This is all I need say of him and his part of the business.

Now, for our part, and the reason why I have called you together. This is what we have done. We have prepared a message for the reigning monarch, his father's brother, who, being an invalid, confined to his bed, is hardly aware of the young man's plans, to ask him to stop him from taking any additional steps in this matter. And we do this because the troops collected, and the various contingents of horse and foot, consist entirely of Norwegians. For this reason, then, we have decided to send you, our faithful friends, Cornelius and Voltimand, to carry our message to the aged monarch, but we grant you only such authority to proceed personally in this matter as the papers herein drawn out expressly permit. Good-bye, and endeavor to show by your speed your attachment to our person.

**Cornelius:** } We will not only prove it in the present case,
**Voltimand:** } but in whatever you bid us do.
**King:** We are quite sure of it, and wish you a cordial good-bye.

[*Exit Voltimand and Cornelius.*]

Well, Laertes, what is this you wish to say to me? I think you said you had some favor to beg. Let me know about it, Laertes. It is impossible for you to make a reasonable request of Denmark's king and waste your words, or to solicit something that I am not ready to grant of my own free will if I only know the nature of it. The various parts of the body are not more naturally or mechanically connected with one another, than are the ruler of this realm and your father. Let me know your wishes, Laertes.

**Laertes:** My revered king, your kind permission to go back to France; for though I came willingly enough from that country to prove my loyalty to you at your enthronement, I am compelled to admit that, having accomplished this task, my desires and wishes draw me thither again, and submit themselves to your generous permission to depart.

**King:** What have you to say upon that subject, Polonius? Has he your permission?

**Polonius:** Yes, your highness, owing to his persistent requests, I have very reluctantly granted it, and finally signified my unwilling approval of his intentions. I earnestly request, therefore, that you will confirm my decision.

**King:** Enjoy then, Laertes, the privileges of youth whilst they last. Remain away as long as you please, and may the fairest accomplishments of which you are master, help you to pass the time in the manner most agreeable to yourself. I must attend, however, to my kinsman, Hamlet, for whom I have now a parental regard.

**Hamlet:** [*Aside.*] Yes, you are more than a mere kinsman to me now; but I hate you nevertheless.

**King:** Why do you continue to preserve such a gloomy aspect?

**Hamlet:** Nay, your highness, I revel in the brightness of your favor.

**Queen:** Hamlet, my son, throw aside your mourning garb, and try to be more favorably disposed toward His Majesty the King. You should not remain for all time gazing with downcast eyes upon the ground as though you were looking for the illustrious parent you have laid there. Death, as you are well aware, is of frequent occurrence, and indeed it is the lot of everything to pass from this life to the life to come.

**Hamlet:** Yes, mother, it occurs frequently enough.

**Queen:** Why, then, does it appear to be something special in your case?

**Hamlet:** Appear, mother? My grief is no mere appearance. My sombre coat, my conventional mourning garb, my noisy stoppages of breath, these are not the only or the true indications of my sorrow. No more are my copious tears, my downcast looks, or any of the other ways and means in which I may outwardly express my grief. The above are undoubtedly appearances, because they may be assumed by anyone at will. I, however, possess something deeper than these, something more than the mere ornamental appendages in which sorrow may be decked.

**King:** The respect you pay to the memory of your dear father, Hamlet, is a pleasant and praiseworthy trait in your character. Still, it should not be forgotten that your father suffered a similar bereavement, and likewise his father before him; the son, in each case, being obliged, by the duty he owed to his parent, to be plunged for a time in grief befitting the occasion. To continue steadfastly in this state, however, is not only cowardly, but an act of irreverent obstinacy. It shows that your disposition is unwilling to submit to divine chastisement, that you have not been strengthened by the consolations of religion to bear up against your loss, but that you foolishly chafe under it like one who has not been taught by experience to endure it bravely.

For surely, when we fretfully oppose and bitterly resent something that is of as frequent occurrence as anything most commonly perceived by us, we wrong not only our Creator and His creation but even the memory of the departed. We also outrage our own understanding, which is perpetually teaching us by every demise that occurs that a parent's death is as usual as it is inevitable.

Cast completely from you then this useless grief, and consider us a father to you, for, we proclaim it openly, you are the next in succession to the crown; and are loved by us with a love as generous as the most affectionate parent could have for his child. As for your proposal of returning to the University of Wittenburg, it is in direct opposition to our wishes, and we earnestly entreat you to be disposed to remain here, that our court may be gladdened and encouraged by the presence of its most distinguished ornament, our dear nephew and son.

**Queen:** Let me not also beg in vain, Hamlet. Remain here with your mother instead of going to Wittenburg.

**Hamlet:** I will do my utmost, mother, to comply with your wishes.

**King:** Well, we could scarcely have expected a more affectionate or reasonable answer. Be one with us here at Elsinore. Come, Gertrude, our son's amiable and voluntary acquiescence is very pleasant and acceptable to me; and, to mark my gratitude for it, every merry toast that we propose this day shall be proclaimed aloud by a burst of artillery. Thus shall the skies resound again and again with the loud reports of the king's revelry. Let us go now.

*[Exit all but Hamlet.]*

**Hamlet:** Would that it were possible for this all too substantial body of mine to liquefy and silently dissipate like the mist of the morning! or that it were not forbidden by divine decree to violently destroy it! Merciful heaven! How tired I am of all the customs of life! How spiritless, tasteless, and useless they appear to me! Bah! The whole earth is in my eyes a neglected garden in which the plants have been left to grow as they please, until it has become entirely occupied by a luxuriant growth of coarse weeds. To think that this should happen! Two short months after his death! No, not even so long as that. And a monarch such as he was; surpassing this one as much as the God of Day surpasses a monster only semihuman; so tenderly regardful of his wife, that he could not even allow the cold blasts too rudely to kiss her face.

Gracious heaven! Why am I compelled to recall these things? She used to cling to him, as if his fond caresses served but to increase her longing for them; and, in spite of all, in less than a month—what would I not give to forget it! Woman, thou art weakness personified! In one short month, before even the shoes were worn out, in which, weeping and inconsolable, she accompanied her husband to his grave, his wife, of all persons—why, a brute entirely without any comprehensive faculty would have felt the loss more keenly—united herself in marriage with his brother, my uncle, a man as unlike him to whom he was so closely related as I am unlike Hercules. In less than a month, before the chafing of that insincere sorrow had ceased to produce redness in her eyes, she rushed with most ungodly willingness and speed into an unholy marriage. Nothing but trouble surely can result from such an alliance; but I must be silent, though my spirit give way under the strain.

[*Enter Horatio, Marcellus and Bernardo.*]

**Horatio:** Greetings to you, my lord!

**Hamlet:** I am pleased to find you in such good health. Horatio, surely, or my eyes are deceiving me!

**Horatio:** It is, your lordship, and he is humbly at your service as he has always been.

**Hamlet:** Call me your friend, Horatio. Let us thus address each other. But why are you not at Wittenburg? Marcellus, too?

**Marcellus:** Your honored lordship—

**Hamlet:** Welcome, sir. I am indeed pleased to greet you. But, let me ask again, what has really brought you from Wittenburg?

**Horatio:** Simply a roving inclination, your lordship.

**Hamlet:** I could not stand idly by while anyone who hated you made such a charge, so you must not compel me to listen to a report like that from your own lips. You have not a roving nature. Tell me, however, your business in Elsinore. We will make a heavy drinker of you before you go away.

**Horatio:** Your lordship, it was the burial of your father which brought me hither.

**Hamlet:** Kindly refrain from making sport of me, Horatio, my friend, and say it was the marriage of my mother.

**Horatio:** Truly, your lordship, they occurred in rapid succession.

**Hamlet:** Economy, my dear fellow! The hot dishes cooked for the funeral were served up cold for the marriage feast. Horatio, I would rather have encountered my bitterest enemy in Paradise than that this should have happened. I can almost fancy I am looking at my dear parent now.

**Horatio:** Tell me where, your lordship.

**Hamlet:** Only in my imagination, Horatio.

**Horatio:** I remember seeing him. He looked every inch a monarch.

**Hamlet:** He possessed such sterling qualities of mind and body, that regarding him from every point of view, I shall never again see his equal.

**Horatio:** Your highness, I believe I beheld him only last night.

**Hamlet:** Whom do you mean?

**Horatio:** The late monarch, your lordship, he of whom we are speaking.

**Hamlet:** He, of whom we are speaking?

**Horatio:** Restrain your astonishment for a few moments, and give me your closest attention, while with my two friends here to support me, I give an account of this remarkable occurrence.

**Hamlet:** Let me know it at once, in the name of all that is holy.

**Horatio:** Twice in succession, whilst they kept guard together in the silent vacancy of midnight, had Marcellus and Bernardo been accosted in the following manner. An apparition, resembling the late king, armed to the smallest detail from head to foot, made its appearance. Three times on each occasion did it stalk past, with solemn step and slow, less than the length of its own baton, from the spot where they stood overpowered and terror-stricken, during which time they, dissolved almost to a jelly by the action of terror upon them, had lost all power of speech. Filled with dread, they told their secret to me, and I, on the following occasion, accompanied them at their post, when at the same time, in the same form, and answering in every particular to their description, the figure appeared. I am familiar with your father's appearance, and it resembled him as closely as these hands resemble each other.

**Hamlet:** Where did this occur, did you say?

**Marcellus:** Before the castle, your highness, where the guard is posted.

**Hamlet:** I suppose you enquired what it wanted?

**Horatio:** Yes, your lordship, but it refused to reply. Still, at one time it raised its eyes and appeared to me to be preparing to speak, but at that very moment, the sound of a cock crowing caused it to start quickly back and disappear from view.

**Hamlet:** This is most remarkable.

**Horatio:** It is a fact, nevertheless, your lordship. I am ready to swear to it. And we considered ourselves under an obligation to tell you about it.

**Hamlet:** Quite right, gentlemen, but this is very disquieting news. Do you keep guard this evening?

**Marcellus:**⎫
**Bernardo:**⎭ Yes, your highness.

**Hamlet:** The figure was in armor, I think you said.

**Marcellus:**⎫
**Bernardo:**⎭ It was, your highness.

**Hamlet:** Completely?

**Marcellus:**⎫
**Bernardo:**⎭ Yes, your highness, to the smallest detail.

**Hamlet:** You could not see how it looked then.

**Horatio:** Certainly we could, your lordship, for his visor was raised.

**Hamlet:** Did he seem displeased?

**Horatio:** No, he appeared to be grieved rather than vexed.

**Hamlet:** Had he a wan or a ruddy look?

**Horatio:** His face was absolutely colorless.

**Hamlet:** And he gazed steadily at you?

**Horatio:** Persistently.

**Hamlet:** I wish I had been present.

**Horatio:** You would have been greatly bewildered.

**Hamlet:** I do not doubt it. How long did it remain?

**Horatio:** Scarcely two minutes.

**Marcellus:**⎫
**Bernardo:**⎭ More than that.

**Horatio:** Not on the occasion I am speaking of.

**Hamlet:** Had his beard a grayish tinge or not?

**Horatio:** It differed in no respect from his appearance before his death; black streaked with gray.

**Hamlet:** I will accompany you tonight at your post in case it again makes its appearance.

**Horatio:** It is sure to do that.

**Hamlet:** Should it come in the likeness of my illustrious parent, hell itself, roaring and bidding me be quiet, shall not prevent me from addressing it. Gentlemen, if you have told no one about this matter up to the present, continue to keep it a secret I beg, and, in addition, whatever besides this may take place while I am with you. Think upon it, but speak not of it, and your devotion will not go unrewarded. Goodbye now. I'll meet you at the appointed place shortly before midnight.

**All:** Your highness may rely upon our faithful obedience to your commands.

**Hamlet:** Say that it is affection rather than duty that prompts your obedience, for I have a sincere regard for you. Good-bye.

[*Exit all but Hamlet.*]

My father rises armed from his tomb. Something is wrong. There has been treachery, I fear. I wish it were time to keep my appointment. Let me curb my suspicions until that moment, for wicked deeds will be discovered however artfully they appear to be concealed.

[*Exit.*]

## ACT I · SCENE 3

[*A room in Polonius' house.*]
[*Enter Laertes and Ophelia.*]

**Laertes:** All that is required for my journey is now safely on board; so good-bye, Ophelia, and whenever the winds are favorable and opportunities of conveyance offer themselves, do not neglect to send me news of your welfare.

**Ophelia:** You know I will.

**Laertes:** With regard to the attention Hamlet is carelessly bestowing upon you, look upon it as a temporary and impulsive fancy of youth, a flower of life's early springtime, premature, but liable soon to decay, pleasant but not enduring; the fragrance and gratification of a moment and nothing besides.

**Ophelia:** Nothing besides that?

**Laertes:** Nothing whatever. Remember that growing nature develops not the body alone, but that the external increase in muscle and stature is accompanied by an internal broadening of the intelligence and feeling. His love may be genuine enough at present whilst his virtuous intentions are unsullied by stain or deceit; but what you have to beware of is that, owing to his high position in the state, he is not master of his own desires, but is under obligations to his kingly origin. He is not permitted, as persons of no distinction are, to cut a way for himself, for the security and well-being of the entire realm are bound up with his selection, and it must therefore be limited by the approval and acquiescence of the people over whom he rules.

So when he declares his passion, you will be discreet if

you trust his promises only so far as his position allows him to fulfil them, and this he can do only when they are in agreement with the wishes of the majority of his subjects. Consider then, what injury you may inflict upon your character, if, being too ready to believe all he says, you surrender your affection to him, or submit yourself to the oft-repeated demands of his unbridled desires.

Be on your guard against this, my beloved sister Ophelia, be on your guard and curb the inclinations of your heart, lest you be carried away by the dangerous assaults of passion. The most scrupulous girl is as lavish with her charms as she ought to be, when she allows even the moon to gaze upon them. Chastity personified is not free from the venomous attacks of slander; and as the young shoots of springtide are blighted by the cankerworm even before their buds have begun to unfold themselves, so in the early dawn of youth, before its freshness has departed from it, infectious blights are most to be feared. Watch, therefore; in flight alone is true security, for even in the absence of a tempter, the passions of youth revolt from the power of self-restraint.

**Ophelia:** Your timely warning shall not fail to make me more watchful for the future over my affections; but, my dear Laertes, do not be like those graceless shepherds who point out to their flocks the dangerous and difficult road to eternal bliss, and at the same time, regardless of their own counsel, and bloated with heedless licentiousness, they themselves dally on the flowery way to destruction.

**Laertes:** Do not be anxious on my behalf. I must be going now; look, however, our father is coming, [*Enter Polonius.*] so as fortune will have it, I am to be honored with the twofold advantage of a second leave-taking.

**Polonius:** Not away, yet, Laertes? Fie upon you, sir. Embark at once, the breeze is already swelling your sails and your companions are waiting for you. Yet, stay a moment to receive my wishes for a successful voyage, and see that you engrave deeply into your remembrance the following maxims. Never say aloud what is in your mind, and do nothing without due deliberation. Mix freely and easily with your acquaintances, but avoid extreme familiarity. Retain by every means in your power, the friends whose loyalty to yourself has ofttimes been proved, but do not make your friendship too common, or think that all who shake you by the hand are united to you in heart. Be not easily provoked to take part in an altercation, but if you do become entangled in one, conduct yourself in such a way that your opponent will feel afraid of commencing another.

Listen attentively to all, but speak to few; and be more fond of receiving than of giving an opinion. Dress as expensively as you can possibly afford, but without undue ostentation, your clothes being costly but not showy. The dress often serves as an indication to the character of the wearer, as the French nobility and gentry know well, who are extremely liberal, especially in matters of dress, and yet have perfect taste. Never request a loan or grant one. Lending money frequently results in the loss, both of the money lent and of the friend to whom it is lent, while getting into debt is one of the chief obstacles to economy. Lastly, and this includes all, always act in a manner worthy of your own ideal. Do this and it will be impossible for you to wrong anyone. Good-bye; and may my regard for your welfare make these warnings the more acceptable to you!

**Laertes:** Your lordship, I bid you a most respectful adieu.

**Polonius:** Away then; the occasion is favorable and your attendants are waiting.

**Laertes:** Good-bye, dear sister, do not forget my counsel.

**Ophelia:** I shall not forget it until I have your express permission to do so.

**Laertes:** Adieu.

*[Exit.]*

**Polonius:** What is this counsel he has been giving you, my daughter?

**Ophelia:** It referred, if you will not be offended by my mentioning it, to Prince Hamlet.

**Polonius:** Good, very opportunely reminded; I have been informed that for some time now, he has passed many of his leisure moments in your company, and that, on your part, you have been exceedingly ready to grant him opportunities. If this is the case—and it has been strongly urged upon me that it is, in a precautionary manner, too—I am bound to let you know that you are not acting with a due consideration of what befits my daughter and her reputation. What mutual understandings have you arrived at? Come, hide nothing from me.

**Ophelia:** I have received lately from him, your lordship, many promises of love.

**Polonius:** Love! Nonsense! You are talking like some silly schoolgirl, without experience in such dangerous matters. You surely put no faith in these so-called promises.

**Ophelia:** I scarcely know what to believe, your lordship.

**Polonius:** Well, let me instruct you. Consider yourself a mere simpleton for thinking that promises such as these have any real value. Consider yourself worth a little more for the future, or, not to stretch the meaning of a phrase too much by using it in this manner, I shall be considered an idiot.

**Ophelia:** But your lordship, he has made genuine proposals of an honest affection for me.

**Polonius:** You do well to say proposals; stuff! nonsense!

**Ophelia:** And has testified his sincerity by almost every possible appeal to the Almighty.

**Polonius:** Yes, snares to trap simpletons. I am aware from experience how lavish one is with solemn promises, when youth and love inflame the blood. But, my dear Ophelia, you must not mistake these flashes of affection for the flame of a true passion. They are more brilliant than enduring, and the vows that accompany them are broken almost before they are uttered. From now on then, see that you give him fewer opportunities of meeting with you, and do not look upon the solicitations you receive as a peremptory offer to entertain his suit.

Finally, with regard to Prince Hamlet, remember that he is still a mere youth, and also that, being a man, he has a considerably larger licence than is permitted to you. In short, Ophelia, put no faith in his promises, for they are not what they seem to be on the surface, but mere go-betweens, negotiators of disgraceful proposals, whispering in pious and sanctimonious tones in order to accomplish more easily their vile purposes. Once for all, I will be quite straightforward with you, you must not again misuse any of your spare time by conversing with Prince Hamlet. See that you obey my commands; go about your business now.

**Ophelia:** Your orders shall be complied with, your lordship.

[*Both exit.*]

# ACT I · SCENE 4

*[The platform.]*
*[Enter Hamlet, Horatio and Marcellus.]*

**Hamlet:** How bitterly cutting the wind feels! It is a severe night.

**Horatio:** Yes, the cold is keen and piercing.

**Hamlet:** I wonder what time it is.

**Horatio:** Almost midnight, I should imagine.

**Hamlet:** That cannot be. The bell sounded that hour some time ago.

**Horatio:** Is that so? I cannot have noticed it. In that case the time is approaching for the apparition to make his accustomed appearance.

*[A flourish of trumpets, and cannons shot off within.]*
Whatever is that noise, your lordship?

**Hamlet:** Our sovereign feasts late this evening, holds a drinking revel and madly treads the steps of the wildest of German dances; and whenever he quaffs a mug of sparkling wine, the unanimous acceptance of his toast is proclaimed abroad by a loud clash of trumpets and drums.

**Horatio:** Is it usual to do this here?

**Hamlet:** Yes, indeed it is; yet I confess that although born and bred in this land, I still regard it as a practice which it is more becoming to ignore than to comply with. These drunken orgies expose us far and wide to the reproof and censure of dwellers in other lands. They say we are a nation of sots, and destroy our reputation by referring to us as "hogs." And more than that, it robs our exploits, even if carried out to the utmost, of the chiefest portion of the praise due to them.

The same thing is true in the case of individuals. One single blemish, sometimes a natural defect which is no fault of their own (no man, for example, can control the circumstances of his birth); sometimes a temperament developing to excess and interfering with the sanity; sometimes an acquired peculiarity destroying the charm of an otherwise pleasing address; one blemish, I repeat, whether natural or accidental, is sufficient to ruin them, and no matter if their other qualities be as perfect as God's abounding favor and as numerous as this mortal nature is able to bear, yet estimated as a whole they will be looked upon as vile. A grain of evil will reduce the purest nature to its own disgraceful level.

[*Enter ghost.*]

**Horatio:** See, your lordship, the apparition approaches.

**Hamlet:** Guard us, holy dispensers of heavenly favor! O specter, whether thou be a righteous soul or an evil one condemned for its wickedness; whether thou comest to me from the pure atmosphere of Paradise or the noxious vapors of Hades; whether thou be benignant or malignant in thy intentions; thy form arouses such questionings in my mind that I cannot be silent. I will appeal to thee by name as my sovereign, my parent, or in any other way that will elicit a reply. Do not suffer me to be overwhelmed by lack of knowledge. Why, O why has thy body which we consigned with due and solemn rites to its last resting place, broken forth from its wrappings? Why has the heavy marble door of the tomb, in which we left thee peacefully interred, burst asunder and refused to confine thee? What can possibly be the reason, O departed one, that thou, clad in full armor, dost once more traverse these earthly shades by moonlight, rendering the hours of darkness so loathsome, that we poor playthings of creation are dreadfully disturbed by questions too profound for our understanding to grasp?

Tell us the meaning of it, and what action you wish us to take.

[*Ghost beckons to Hamlet.*]

**Horatio:** It motions you to retire in its company, so, seemingly, it has some message to communicate to you privately.

**Marcellus:** Notice how politely it beckons you to accompany it to a more retired spot. Pay no heed to it, however.

**Horatio:** Certainly not, on any account.

**Hamlet:** As it will say nothing to me here, I must obey.

**Horatio:** Let me beg your lordship not to.

**Hamlet:** Tell me, is there anything to be afraid of? I value my existence at the merest trifle, and it cannot possibly harm my spirit which is as imperishable as it is. Once more it beckons me. I must accompany it.

**Horatio:** Supposing, your lordship, it should entice you to the water's edge, or to the topmost crag of yonder precipice which juts frowningly toward the ocean, and then put on a shape so hideous that at the sight of it your mind loses its controlling principle and you are left insane? Consider now! No further inducement is necessary beyond the spot itself to fill with headstrong fancies the minds of all who stand at such a height gazing downwards at the ocean and listening to the raging tumult below.

**Hamlet:** It continues to beckon me. Lead the way and I will come.

**Marcellus:** We cannot allow it, your lordship.

**Hamlet:** Leave me alone.

**Horatio:** Submit yourselves to our control in this matter, your lordship. We must prevent you.

**Hamlet:** My destiny urges me onward, causing every tiny fiber in my frame to become as strong as the sinews of the lion which Hercules killed. It is summoning me yet. Hands off, sirs. I swear I will slay anyone who hinders me now. Keep off, I tell you! Lead the way. I am coming.

[*Exit ghost and Hamlet.*]

**Horatio:** His excited fancy makes him more and more rash.

**Marcellus:** We must go after him. We should not heed his commands in this case.

**Horatio:** Let us go then. What will be the result of this?

**Marcellus:** There is something radically wrong with our country.

**Horatio:** We must leave the result to Providence.

**Marcellus:** No, it would be better to go after him.

[*All exit.*]

## ACT I · SCENE 5

[*Another part of the platform.*]
[*Enter ghost and Hamlet.*]

**Hamlet:** Where do you wish to take me? Tell me. This is as far as I will go.

**Ghost:** Hearken to my word.

**Hamlet:** I am listening.

**Ghost:** My moments are but few, and then I must return to agonizing fires of burning brimstone.

**Hamlet:** Unhappy spirit! Your sorrows excite my sympathy.

**Ghost:** Nay, waste not compassionate words upon me, but pay careful attention to the information I am about to disclose.

**Hamlet:** Say on, my duty compels me to listen.

**Ghost:** It will likewise compel you to avenge after you have

19

listened.

**Hamlet:** Avenge?

**Ghost:** Hamlet, the ghost of your dead parent stands before you, condemned for a stated time to spend its nights in wandering about, and its days imprisoned in penitential flames, until by their purifying action, the wicked deeds of my earthly days are completely atoned for. Were it not that I am compelled to remain silent concerning the nature of my place of correction, I could give an account, the most trifling detail of which would acutely distress your mind, congeal your youthful blood, cause your organs of vision to shoot wildly from their orbits like meteors, and each individual hair of your matted and tangled ringlets to spring up and remain erect, as the spikes of the porcupine do when that animal is irritated. This revelation of the mysteries of the other world is, however, denied to mortal man. Listen to me now! If your affection for your loving parent was ever genuine—

**Hamlet:** Do you doubt it?

**Ghost:** You will not allow the vile and inhuman monster to escape who took my life.

**Hamlet:** Took your life!

**Ghost:** Ay, committed a crime which is the vilest of all, even in cases where there is some provocation, but in my case especially vile, unusual, and inhuman.

**Hamlet:** Acquaint me quickly with the circumstances, so that almost before I have time to think of it, I may rush like a whirlwind to wreak vengeance upon the criminal.

**Ghost:** I am glad you are so ready, and indeed you would be more slothful than the rank vegetation whose slow growth fringes the River of Forgetfulness, did this not move you. Listen, then, Hamlet. It is said that my death was caused by a venomous snake biting me while I slumbered in my garden, and in this way the entire population of this country has been fooled by an entirely fictitious account of the matter. The truth is, my worthy son, that the reptile to whom I owe my death has now stepped into my place.

**Hamlet:** My uncle! This explains my distrust of him!

**Ghost:** Yes, that brute, violating every principle of chastity and fidelity, by the exercise of all the cunning devices which his wisdom and abilities could suggest (sinful indeed must they be to accomplish such ends) treacherously charmed into compliance with his depraved desires your mother, so faithful to all appearances. What a base desertion was this, my son, to forsake me whose affection for her was so worthy that it never violated in the slightest degree the promises I made to her at the altar, and to stoop to a base creature like this, whose innate abilities will not suffer comparison with mine! But, just as a truly chaste person could never be seduced, even were the tempter to assume an angelic form, so marriage with a celestial being would not effect a lasting change upon one really sensual, who, after filling himself to repletion with the companionship of the purest of saints, would hanker after garbage.

Enough of this, however. I fancy I feel the dawn approaching, and must therefore proceed quickly with my story. Whilst enjoying, then, my usual afternoon slumber in the garden, my brother crept toward me bearing a small vessel containing a poisonous extraction of henbane, and in my unguarded state he filled the entrances of my ears with the contents. This leprosy-producing distillation no sooner enters the blood stream than, rushing swiftly through the veins and arteries, it permeates the whole system, and with a rapid and violent action causes the healthy blood, usually a mobile fluid, to curdle and clot just as milk does when acted upon by an acid. Such was the result in my case. The entire surface of my smooth skin became almost immediately coated with a thick incrustation, a vile and hateful covering, resembling leprosy.

In this way, then, did my brother in my slumber deprive me at the same instant of all that was dearest to me—wife, sovereignty, and existence itself. In this way did he bring my career to an abrupt conclusion in the very full bloom of my wickedness. Without the Sacrament, without preparation, without Extreme Unction and without in any way having made my peace with my Heavenly Father, but bearing on my own person the full weight of all my shortcomings, I was hurried into the Divine presence, there to answer for my sins. What an awful, dreadful, loathsome act! If you have any natural feelings whatever, do not endure it, do not allow the home of Denmark's king to be disgraced by such lewd and hateful lust. But in whatever way you carry out your purpose, act in a straightforward manner, and do not plot to injure your mother. Let her punishment come from above and from the pangs and twinges of her own conscience. I must say good-bye at this very moment, for I perceive by the dimness and uselessness of the glow-worm's light that morning approaches. Farewell, a last farewell; do not forget my wrongs.

[Exit ghost.]

**Hamlet:** Throng to my aid, ye dwellers in celestial heights and ye terrestrial powers also! What others shall I invoke? The spirits of darkness? Perish the thought! O heart, slow thy tumultuous beating! O limbs, support me firmly upon my feet; let not thy muscles grow suddenly too feeble to bear me. Forget thy wrongs, dear father! Impossible, so long as my brain, perplexed with doubts and fears, is capable of performing its functions. More than that, from my storehouse of knowledge, I'll eject every foolish and trifling fact, every copybook maxim, every past impression and observation gathered in my youthful days, so that thy injunction, and that only, may hold absolute sway within the range and compass of my understanding, to the exclusion of all less important matters. Yea, I have sworn it! Who would have believed it? The deadly sin of the wife! The cursed and plausible rascality of her paramour!

Where is my memorandum book? It befits me to make a note of it. A plausible manner may cloak a wicked heart. 'Tis true at any rate in this part of the world. [*Writing.*] Now, uncle, I have it down against you. Let me recall again my father's injunction. Farewell! do not forget my wrongs. My oath is taken.

**Marcellus:** } [*Within.*] Are you there, your lordship?
**Horatio:**

**Marcellus:** [*Within.*] Our gracious prince!
**Horatio:** [*Within.*] May the Lord keep him from all harm!
**Hamlet:** Amen.
**Horatio:** [*Within.*] Hello, ho, ho, your lordship!
**Hamlet:** Hello, ho, ho, my bird! Come quickly.

[Enter Horatio and Marcellus.]

**Marcellus:** Is all well with your highness?
**Horatio:** What did it tell you, your lordship?
**Hamlet:** Surprising news.

**Horatio:** Let us hear it, gracious prince.

**Hamlet:** I cannot; I do not wish it to become known.

**Horatio:** I swear to maintain secrecy.

**Marcellus:** And I, too, your lordship.

**Hamlet:** Well, what do you think? Is it possible even so much as to conceive such a tale? But you are sure it will go no farther?

**Horatio:**
**Marcellus:** } You have our solemn promise, your lordship.

**Hamlet:** It is impossible to find a rogue in the whole of this land who is not a downright rascal.

**Horatio:** I am sure, your lordship, that we do not require a messenger from the dead to acquaint us with that fact.

**Hamlet:** I must say that your remark is perfectly just. Therefore, to be quite straightforward with you, I think we had better take leave of each other in a friendly manner and go our several ways; you in whatever direction your duty or inclination prompts, for you must have one or the other, whatever they may be. With regard to my own humble self, mark you, I shall betake myself to prayer.

**Horatio:** This is mere thoughtless, extravagant speech, your lordship.

**Hamlet:** I deeply regret that it displeases you; in very truth, I sincerely regret it.

**Horatio:** You need have no regrets, your lordship.

**Hamlet:** You are wrong, Horatio, for I swear I have a great deal to regret. With regard to this apparition, however, I give you my word that it is no lying spirit. At the same time, I must ask you to stifle, as best you can, your curiosity concerning its interview with me. Now, my dear companions, on your word as companions, fellow students, and comrades in arms, grant me this tiny petition.

**Horatio:** We promise to do so, your lordship, whatever it may be.

**Hamlet:** Tell no one of the events you have witnessed this night.

**Horatio:**
**Marcellus:** } Your lordship, we give you our word.

**Hamlet:** Yes, but I require your oath.

**Horatio:** By my troth, my lordship, I will not.

**Marcellus:** I will not, your lordship, by my troth.

**Hamlet:** Take an oath to that effect upon the hilt of my sword.

**Marcellus:** Your lordship, we have just taken an oath.

**Hamlet:** Yes, but take it in the formal manner I have described.

**Ghost:** [*Beneath.*] Obey.

**Hamlet:** Ha, ha, old fellow! Did you speak? What do you there, my honest fellow? Now, gentlemen, you see I am supported by a friend underground. Agree to take the oath.

**Horatio:** Administer it then, your lordship.

**Hamlet:** You solemnly promise with your hand upon this weapon that you will tell no one of what has happened.

**Ghost:** [*Beneath.*] Promise.

**Hamlet:** Why, he's here and everywhere. Let us once more change our position. This way, my friends; place your hands upon the hilt of my sword and solemnly promise that you will tell no one of what has happened tonight. Come promise.

**Ghost:** [*Beneath.*] Promise.

**Hamlet:** An opportune remark, my burrowing friend. You are a first-class earth worker, I perceive, and would make an excellent pioneer. Another change of ground, gentlemen.

**Horatio:** I call heaven to witness if this is not amazingly surprising!

**Hamlet:** As it is surprising then, believe it without question. The universe contains many wonders that the science you are addicted to has never even imagined as yet. But to the oath. You give me your word in this place as you did over there, that if it should suit my purpose on some future occasion to conduct myself in a fantastic manner, you will never, as you hope for divine clemency, however strangely or curiously I may behave, give the slightest hint that you have any inkling as to the cause of it either by folding your arms thus, or knowingly nodding your head or using such ambiguous expressions as "If we only cared to tell," "We could explain if we wished to," "If it only suited us to speak," "We know some who could if they were allowed to," or any other of a like nature. Promise this, and take an oath that divine favor and clemency may desert you in your hour of greatest necessity if you should break it.

**Ghost:** [*Beneath.*] Promise.

**Hamlet:** Slumber in peace, disturbed one. [*They swear.*] Now, friends, let me take leave, sincerely avowing my affectionate regard for you, and as much as it is possible for me in my humble position to do to prove my affection and friendship for you, I promise that, if God so please, it shall not be wanting. We had better go now, and let me again urge you to a perpetual silence. Matters in this age are completely disorganized. Oh, the bitter irony of fate that has ordained me, of all persons, to restore them to order! Stay, I am coming with you.

[*Exit.*]

# ACT II · SCENE 1

*[A room in Polonius' house.]*
*[Enter Polonius and Reynaldo.]*

**Polonius:** I want you to carry, Reynaldo, this gold and these written instructions to my son.

**Reynaldo:** I will see that he receives them, your lordship.

**Polonius:** It will certainly be an act of much wisdom on your part, my dear Reynaldo, if you endeavor to find out how he has been conducting himself.

**Reynaldo:** Such was my purpose, your lordship.

**Polonius:** I am glad to hear you say so, exceedingly glad. Hearken, then. To begin with, find out on my behalf what countrymen of ours are staying in Paris, their manner of life, who they are, the part of the city in which they dwell and their financial circumstances; what class of people they entertain and the style in which they entertain them. By discovering in this winding and circuitous manner that they are acquainted with Laertes, you will get much nearer to the subject than you could possibly do by direct questioning. Now assume the appearance of having a slight acquaintance with him; say "I am on rather intimate terms with his father and his companions, and have been introduced to him, too." Do you follow me, Reynaldo?

**Reynaldo:** Perfectly, your lordship.

**Polonius:** "I have been introduced to him;" still, be careful to add, "my acquaintance with him is but slight; nevertheless, if he is the person I am referring to, he is a rather fast young man, much given to this and that," and here you may attribute to him what imaginary vices you can think fit, but mind, not such grave ones as would disgrace him— be careful in that respect—but the ordinary careless and extravagant lapses from strict morality that are known to be generally associated with a young man not under parental control.

**Reynaldo:** Gambling, for instance, your lordship.

**Polonius:** Yes, or drinking, brawling, cursing, squabbling. I think you may venture to mention these.

**Reynaldo:** Surely, your lordship, these would disgrace him.

**Polonius:** Not at all, so long as you qualify them in the telling. Do not, however, impute to him the graver charge that he is unable to bridle his passions. I do not wish you to understand that; yet utter all his faults with such artful reservations that people may look upon them as mere blemishes arising from his being his own master, fiery outbursts of a high spirit, a wildness of undisciplined nature to which all young men are liable.

**Reynaldo:** Will your lordship tell me—

**Polonius:** Why I wish you to do this?

**Reynaldo:** Yes, your lordship. That is what I intended to say.

**Polonius:** Well, Reynaldo, this is what I am driving at, and I think it is an artifice that will be found effective in practice. When you speak in this way of my boy, comparing him to an article slightly damaged by usage, do you see, if the person with whom you are speaking, and from whom you wish to obtain some information, has actually observed the young man you are referring to engaged in the above-mentioned acts, he will agree with you in such words as these, "My dear sir," or something of that sort, "My friend" or "My lord," according to your title and the mode of address common in that land.

**Reynaldo:** I understand, your lordship.

**Polonius:** After that, Reynaldo—goodness. Surely I have not forgotten what I wished to say. Dear me, I must have intended to make some remarks. What did I say last?

**Reynaldo:** He agrees with you in such words as these, and "My friend" and "My lord."

**Polonius:** Of course. He agrees with you in such words as these, that was it. He agrees by saying, "I am acquainted with the young man, and I have seen him on several occasions quite recently with this person and that person, and, as you remarked, he was gambling at one time, the worse for drink at another, quarrelling over a game of tennis at a third;" and, he may even add, "I noticed him the other day going into a house of ill fame," or something like that.

You see now, the false vices you attribute to him, serve to reveal his real failings. It is in this way that we who are wise and shrewd, by winding and indirect courses, like the curved path of a bowl towards the jack, arrive at the truth. And in this way will you, if you follow the advice I have just given, find out about my son. You quite understand me, I trust.

**Reynaldo:** I do, your lordship.

**Polonius:** Heaven guard you on your way! Farewell.

**Reynaldo:** I thank your lordship.

**Polonius:** Do not be content to enquire; find out by personal observation to what he is addicted.

**Reynaldo:** Very well, your lordship.

**Polonius:** Let him follow his own bent, however.

**Reynaldo:** I shall, your lordship.

**Polonius:** Good-bye.

[*Exit Reynaldo.*]
[*Enter Ophelia.*]

You here, Ophelia! Whatever is wrong?

**Ophelia:** Oh, father, I am nearly dead with terror.

**Polonius:** With terror! Let me beseech you to explain.

**Ophelia:** Your lordship, whilst employed with my needle in my own room, Prince Hamlet entered. His coat was entirely unfastened, his head uncovered, and his stockings, begrimed with dirt, hung down like fetters about his ankles. His face was deadly white, and the expression of his countenance betokened so much misery that he seemed as if he had just escaped from Hades, and had come to tell me of the terrible sights he had just witnessed there.

**Polonius:** Driven to distraction by his passion for you?

**Ophelia:** I cannot tell your lordship, but such I am afraid was the case.

**Polonius:** What words did he speak?

**Ophelia:** He grasped me tightly by the wrist and, retreating as far as his arm would allow, he shaded his eyes with his unoccupied palm in this fashion, and made a thorough study of my face as if he intended to paint my picture. He remained a considerable time in this position, but finally, after causing my arm to tremble slightly, and nodding his head several times like this, he sighed so deeply and mournfully that the whole of his body appeared to fall to pieces under its influence, and I thought he was done for. After that he released his hold and, gazing all the while at me over his shoulder, he made his way out of the room without the assistance of his eyes, for, until the moment of his departure, they were turned in my direction.

**Polonius:** Let us go to his majesty together, at once. This is exactly the kind of madness that results from affection unrequited. Love is so furious in its action that it often destroys itself and drives its victims to distraction, more frequently than any other violent feeling to which our frail dispositions are prone. This grieves me very much. You must have replied harshly of late to his entreaties.

**Ophelia:** My dear father, I did nothing more than obey your orders by rejecting his communications and refusing to allow him to see me.

**Polonius:** And his insanity is the result. I deeply regret now that I did not exercise more observation and care in forming my opinion of him. I thought he was only toying with your affections, and intended to ruin you. Curse my suspicion, but still it is the failing of my time of life; excess of caution is just as characteristic of men of experience, as lack of caution is of the young and inexperienced. However, we must see his majesty. I must make him acquainted with our discovery, for though I may excite his resentment by telling him of Hamlet's regard for you, greater sorrow would certainly come from concealing it. Let us go.

[*Exit.*]

## ACT II · SCENE 2

[*A room in the castle.*]
[*Enter king, queen, Rosencrantz,
Guildenstern and attendants.*]

**King:** Rosencrantz and Guildenstern, our good friends, we are pleased to see you. Beside the fact that we greatly desired to have you with us again, we must confess that our sudden summons is due to the fact that your presence will be very useful to us just now. I suppose you are aware of the complete change that has taken place in our son of late. I say complete change, for both in body and mind he is totally unlike his natural self. The probable cause of this complete alienation from all knowledge of his former self is beyond my powers of conception, unless it be grief for the loss of his parent. I therefore beg that you two, who have been his companions from his very childhood, and are consequently intimately associated with his youthful disposition, will condescend to stay with us at Elsinore a few days, so that you may induce him to take his amusements along with you, and pick up, as far as opportunity will allow, any information you can on the subject of his malady, whether it is anything of which we are at present ignorant and could remove if it were only known.

**Queen:** Worthy sirs, you are frequently the subject of his conversation, and it is my firm opinion that we could not find another pair of companions to whom he is more devotedly attached. Should you think fit to prove your courtesy and kind feeling by abiding here awhile to aid and further our desires, you will be thanked for your visit in a truly royal manner.

**Rosencrantz:** It shows great condescension on the part of our king and queen to make this request of us, since the absolute sway they exercise over our persons entitles them to signify their desires, too awful for a subject to disobey, in a peremptory form.

**Guildenstern:** Nevertheless, we are just as ready to carry them out, and we now place our utmost energies entirely at your disposal, and are willing to obey humbly whatever order it pleases you to give.

**King:** We are obliged to you, Rosencrantz, and to you, our amiable friend, Guildenstern.

**Queen:** I am also obliged to you, Guildenstern, and to you, our amiable friend, Rosencrantz, and I earnestly request that you will immediately pay your respects to my boy, who has undergone such a sad transformation. Will one or two of you kindly usher our friends into Hamlet's presence?

**Guildenstern:** God grant that our companionship may be agreeable, and our conduct of some assistance to him.

**Queen:** Yes, may it be so!

> [*Exit Rosencrantz, Guildenstern and some*
> *attendants.*]
> [*Enter Polonius.*]

**Polonius:** The envoys you dispatched, your highness, have come back with the glad news that their mission has been a complete success.

**King:** You seem to be fated to bring nothing but joyful tidings into my presence.

**Polonius:** Indeed, your highness, I can positively assert that I look upon my immortal spirit and faithful services, just as sacred trusts, one to my Maker and the other to our illustrious monarch. And I believe that I have discovered the true reason for the madness of your son, unless that is, my mind is not so adept as it was once at tracing results to their very source.

**King:** Let me know it at once, for that is the matter above all others, about which I thirst for information.

**Polonius:** Wait until you have seen the envoys and heard the result of your mission, and let my information serve as a fitting finale to the pleasure which you will derive from the message of which they are the bearers.

**King:** Honor them then, by personally conducting them into our presence.

*[Exit Polonius.]*

Did you hear him say, sweet Queen, how he has discovered the true origin from which Hamlet's derangement springs?

**Queen:** I am afraid he can find no other cause but the chief one, the death of his parent and our precipitate union.

**King:** At any rate, we'll question him closely and find out.

*[Re-enter Polonius, with Voltimand and Cornelius.]*

Congratulations upon your return, my loving subjects. Well, Voltimand, what answer have you received from our fellow sovereign, the Norwegian king?

**Voltimand:** He not only reciprocates your salutations, but complies with all your wishes. As soon as he heard us, he gave orders that the troops collected by his young kinsman should be disbanded. Indeed, he would never have consented to their collection had he not been under the impression that they were to be used against the Poles. Upon closer inquiry, however, he discovered that they were, without doubt, to be used against your majesty, and it angered him so much to find that his nephew had taken advantage of his illness, advancing years and general debility to delude him, that he summoned him at once to his presence. The young man speedily appeared, was severely scolded by him and, in the end, pledged his word never again to put his quarrel against your highness to the test of war.

The aged king was so delighted at this that he promised him three thousand crowns a year and gave him permission to use the troops he had mustered against the Poles. We therefore bear a request, which is stated here in full,

31

[*Giving a paper*] that you will assist his expedition by allowing him to march peacefully through your realm, on the conditions stated on the paper, that the country will be free from all danger while the troops are passing.

**King:** We are very pleased with this answer, and at a more suitable time for deliberation we will peruse the paper and, after careful thought, make our reply thereto. Till then, accept our thanks for the admirable way in which you have conducted the mission. Retire now and this evening we will hold a banquet in your honor. Meanwhile, accept our hearty greetings on your return.

[*Exit Voltimand and Cornelius.*]

**Polonius:** This matter is now satisfactorily concluded. My sovereign lord and lady, an adequate discussion of the essential characteristics of royal dignity or the nature of duty, or a consideration of the reasons for light and darkness, and time itself, being what they are, would be merely a useless expenditure of the things thus named. Since, then, it is the very essence of wisdom to be concise, and seeing that all tiresome circumlocutions are but surface embellishments and appendages to it, I intend to be concise. Prince Hamlet is a madman. I say a madman, for all the definitions of insanity amount in brief to this, that insanity consists of being insane. We'll let that pass, however.

**Queen:** Put more substance into your remarks and couch them in a less florid style.

**Polonius:** I pledge my word, my sovereign lady, that I have no intention of cloaking facts with specious explanations. He is undoubtedly insane. Indeed, to make use of a rather silly rhetorical device, I regret that it is a fact, and the fact is regrettable. Granting, then, it be proved that he is insane, we have still to discover what has brought on this state of mind, or better still this loss of mind, for there must be some reason for its imperfection. This is what is still left for our consideration. Consider it carefully then. My child, who may be said to belong to me as long as I retain my hold upon her, has loyally complied with my instructions and brought this to me. Kindly listen to, and ponder over these words: [*Reads.*] "To the object of my heart's adoration, the seraphic and beautified Ophelia." "Beautified" is an unsuitable adjective—a most shockingly unsuitable adjective—but let us proceed. Listen, then: [*Reads.*] "I address these letters hoping that she may treasure them within her breast of snowy whiteness."

**Queen:** Do you mean to tell me that Hamlet wrote this to her?

**Polonius:** Have patience a moment, your majesty. I will omit nothing. [*Reads.*] "Though you may have a misgiving that the stars are, after all, mere specks of flame, and that the orb of day is not stationary; though your faith in truth itself may be severely shaken, never disbelieve for one moment that my affections are centered in you alone. O Ophelia, my loved one, I am a poor hand at this sort of work, and am utterly unable adequately to express in verse the moanings of my love; be assured, nevertheless, that I do adore you beyond all else. Farewell. Eternally yours, well beloved one, Whilst this body remains his own, Hamlet."

Ophelia has not only dutifully brought this to me, but, in addition, has given me privately a full account of all his courtship, whenever, wherever, and however it took place.

**King:** Well, how did the lady treat these amorous advances?

**Polonius:** What is your opinion of my character?

**King:** I believe you to be motivated by true and lofty principles.

**Polonius:** And it is my wish to sustain this reputation. Would, however, your opinion have remained the same if, after I had noticed how fiercely his passion urged him onward, and I did notice it, let me tell you, before I was informed of it, would your opinion have remained the same, I say, or that of her beloved highness, your consort, if I had kept the knowledge to myself, as if it were locked up in a desk or memorandum book, or if I had silently connived at it, or even carelessly thought little or nothing about it? Would it have been the same?

Certainly not. I interfered at once, and without ceremony addressed my youthful daughter somewhat in this fashion: Prince Hamlet is of royal blood, belongs to a sphere quite beyond you, and, therefore, all thought of courtship with him must cease. I then immediately charged her to shut herself entirely from those places where she would be likely to meet him, to send back anyone whom he might send to her, and refuse all his presents. My daughter, having heard, profited by the counsel, and to put it briefly, the poor young man, his advances being thus checked, sank into a state of melancholy and refused to take food. This was followed by sleeplessness, debility and light-headedness, and thus by gradual degrees he lapsed into this state of insanity which now afflicts him and grieves us all so much.

**King:** Can this really be the case?

**Queen:** It is possible, even probable.

**Polonius:** Tell me, if you can, have you even known me to say definitely that such and such was true and found that I was mistaken?

**King:** I do not remember any occasion.

**Polonius:** [*Pointing to his head and shoulders.*] Well, may these be severed if I am not right this time. If I have any clues to guide me, I will discover the true facts of a case, even should they be concealed in the very middle of the earth.

**King:** What other way is there of testing your theory?

**Polonius:** You are aware that he has a habit of strolling about the hall for long periods at a time, are you not?

**Queen:** I have often noticed it.

**Polonius:** Well then, on one of these occasions I will place Ophelia so that he may encounter her, whilst you and I, concealing ourselves behind the tapestry, will take special notice of the interview. Should I be mistaken, and his passion has not unhinged his mind, I am willing to give up statecraft altogether and go in for agriculture.

**King:** We will do as you suggest.

**Queen:** Hush, here comes the poor unhappy fellow himself, mournfully poring over a book.

**Polonius:** Leave him alone with me, I beg of you, and I'll accost him immediately.

[*Exit king, queen and attendants.*]
[*Enter Hamlet, reading.*]

Pardon my interruption, my lord, but may I enquire how your highness is keeping?

**Hamlet:** I am in excellent health, thank God.

**Polonius:** Is your lordship acquainted with me?

**Hamlet:** Perfectly, my dear sir. You are a fish dealer.

**Polonius:** Indeed, your lordship, but you're mistaken.

**Hamlet:** Well, I wish you had as much integrity as one.

**Polonius:** Integrity, did you say?

**Hamlet:** Yes, integrity, for not more than one man in a

thousand conforms even to this world's poor standard of integrity.

**Polonius:** Indeed, your lordship, but that is so.

**Hamlet:** For just as the sun divine may bathe with its rays the dead and putrid flesh of a dog, and cause life to spring therefrom—You have a child, I believe?

**Polonius:** Yes, your highness.

**Hamlet:** See that she is not allowed to go unrestrained. Understanding is a blessing, but she may understand too much. Be careful, my dear sir.

**Polonius:** [*Aside.*] What do you think of that now? My child again! She seems forever on his mind. Still, he must be very mad. He did not even recognize me at first, but took me for a fish dealer. In faith, when I was a young fellow, I too endured the severest pangs of this amorous passion, almost as bad as this. I'll try him once more. What are you studying, your lordship?

**Hamlet:** Nothing but mere words.

**Polonius:** And what is it about?

**Hamlet:** What is what about?

**Polonius:** The book you are studying, your lordship.

**Hamlet:** It is very libellous, sir. The author here abuses old men shamefully. He not only rails at their snow-white hair, furrowed countenances, but adds that their eyes exude a yellowish discharge, that their wisdom is conspicuous by its absence, and that their knee joints are too feeble to support them. And though these statements may be true, indeed I am firmly convinced that they are, still I think it very ungentlemanly conduct to put them into writing, for you yourself, sir, would be as old as I am, that is, if you could imitate the crab and retrace your steps.

**Polonius:** [*Aside.*] Well, his remarks may be insane, but they are not without a certain order and arrangement. Will you come outside with me, your lordship?

**Hamlet:** Yes, I'll go to my tomb.

**Polonius:** True enough, he would have to go outside to do that. [*Aside.*] His retorts are often extremely appropriate. People in his condition appear indeed to stumble upon felicitous modes of expression, which seem unattainable to persons in full possession of their faculties. I'll take my departure now, and see if I cannot arrange matters at once so that he may encounter Ophelia.—Most illustrious Prince, I respectfully beg that you will give me permission to depart.

**Hamlet:** There is nothing I have, sir, that I could give with better grace than that, with the exception of my existence. Yes, my existence.

**Polonius:** Good-bye, then, your lordship.

**Hamlet:** How these venerable dotards bore me.

*[Enter Rosencrantz and Guildenstern.]*

**Polonius:** If you are looking for Prince Hamlet, you will find him here.

**Rosencrantz:** *[To Polonius.]* Greeting to you, my lord.

*[Exit Polonius.]*

**Guildenstern:** My revered prince!

**Rosencrantz:** My beloved prince!

**Hamlet:** My highly esteemed comrades! How are you, Guildenstern? How are you, Rosencrantz? How are you both, my dear fellows?

**Rosencrantz:** As well as ordinary beings like ourselves expect to be.

**Guildenstern:** We are fortunate enough not to enjoy perfect happiness. We are not specially favored by the Fates.

**Hamlet:** Nor especially hated, I presume.

**Rosencrantz:** No, your lordship.

**Hamlet:** Then you occupy the middle station between these two extremes. Tell me the latest tidings.

**Rosencrantz:** There is nothing to tell, my lord, except that everyone has become strictly honorable nowadays.

**Hamlet:** The Judgment Day must be close at hand then; but I cannot believe that. Excuse me for troubling you with a question of a more personal nature. What special grudge does fortune owe you that she has brought you to a jail like this?

**Guildenstern:** A jail, your highness!

**Hamlet:** Yes, a jail like Denmark.

**Rosencrantz:** If you call Denmark a jail, you must call the whole earth one too.

**Hamlet:** So it is, and a very large jail, which contains many places of imprisonment, divisions and cells, few of which are so bad as this country.

**Rosencrantz:** That is not our opinion, your lordship.

**Hamlet:** Well, then, to you it is not a prison at all; our surroundings are just what our imaginations make of them. I look upon it as such.

**Rosencrantz:** If you feel imprisoned in Denmark, it must be on account of your desire for power. So small a country does not offer sufficient scope for conceptions like yours.

**Hamlet:** You are wrong there, sir, for were it not for the visions that disturb my slumbers, I could fancy myself a monarch of boundless sway, with a kingdom no larger than a nut.

**Guildenstern:** This proves that we are correct, for what are those who thirst after power constantly striving to obtain, except something as unreal as the ghost of a vision?

**Hamlet:** Even a vision is unreal.

**Rosencrantz:** And indeed, consider the thirst after power a thing so short-lived that it is the mere reflection of something unreal.

**Hamlet:** In that case, then, the only true substantial men are beggars, for they alone do not seek power, and, seeing that what they seek has no real existence, great kings and strutting warriors who seek it are merely the reflections of beggars. Let us go to the king's presence now, for, in faith, this subject is too deep for my understanding.

**Rosencrantz:** } We desire only to serve you.
**Guildenstern:** }

**Hamlet:** Not at all. I would not allow you to associate with my other attendants for, to tell you the truth, they are not a pleasant lot. But to use my licence as a friend and speak bluntly to you, why have you come to Elsinore?

**Rosencrantz:** For no other reason, your highness, than to pay our respects to you.

**Hamlet:** So poor am I that I cannot even be generous with my expressions of gratitude. Still I desire to express it, but I am afraid, my good comrades, that my gratitude in this instance is worthless. Did you come of your own accord? Is there no motive for your visit? Did nobody ask you to come? Be frank and fair with me now, and tell the truth. Don't be afraid. Speak out.

**Guildenstern:** What reason could we possibly give if we did speak, your lordship?

**Hamlet:** Any reason but the true one. You have been asked to come. I can see it in your faces, whose expression you are too natural to be able completely to control. I am certain that you have been requested to come by their gracious majesties.

**Rosencrantz:** For what purpose, your highness?

**Hamlet:** Nay, I'll leave that for you to tell me. I charge you, however, by the claims I have upon you as a comrade, by the memory of the youthful days we spent together, by the duty you owe to our steadily maintained affection, and by whatever else stronger than these a more eloquent advocate than myself might provide on my behalf, to be straightforward with me, and tell me plainly if it is true that you were asked to come.

**Rosencrantz:** [*Aside to Guildenstern.*] Shall we tell him?

**Hamlet:** [*Aside.*] Be careful now, I'm watching you. Come, if you really care for me still, do not hesitate to tell me.

**Guildenstern:** Well, then, we were requested to come.

**Hamlet:** Let me tell you the reason. By so doing, I will render your disclosure of it needless, and thus the promise you made to their majesties not to divulge it need not be broken. For some time past I have, without being able to account for it, become greatly changed. I am no longer joyous! I have given up my usual practice of manly accomplishments and, in fact, my natural tendency is so severely shaken that this fair world of ours is in my eyes a dreary waste; its splendid covering, the atmosphere, mark you, the beautiful sky which embraces it, the stately vault of the heavens embossed and adorned with flames of gold, is in my sight nothing more than a collection of loathesome and noxious gases.

Man himself, that monument of creative skill, endowed with such magnificence of intellect, such immensity of ability, in figure and carriage so astonishingly and exactly fitted to his purpose, resembling a celestial being in his exploits, and a very deity in his conceptions, the flower of the whole earth and the grand ideal of all animate nature— even he, the highest perfection attainable by earthly matter, ceases any more to afford me pleasure; neither does his consort, though from your looks you seem to disbelieve me.

**Rosencrantz:** I never for one moment entertained such an idea, your lordship.

**Hamlet:** What caused you to smile then, when I told you that I took no pleasure in man?

**Rosencrantz:** The thought of the meager reception the actors will get at the hands of one "who takes no pleasure in man." We caught up to them as we were coming, and they intend to come here to see if you will engage them.

**Hamlet:** I will give worthy reception to him who takes the regal part, the monarch shall receive due homage from me; the knight-errant will have the opportunity of showing his prowess with sword and buckler, the sighs of the lovesick swain will not be wasted, the capricious gentleman will not be prevented from saying all his lines; the antics of the fool will afford much merriment to those who are easily moved to laughter; and the lady will spoil the meter rather than not express herself freely. Who are these actors?

**Rosencrantz:** The same that you used to be so fond of hearing; the town players.

**Hamlet:** But what has caused them to become itinerant? They would surely advance more both in wealth and public estimation by performing in a fixed place.

**Rosencrantz:** I think they have been compelled to leave the city owing to the popularity of the latest theatrical fashion.

**Hamlet:** Is their reputation as good as it was when I was in the habit of seeing them? Do they still draw such large audiences?

**Rosencrantz:** In truth, sir, I am afraid they do not.

**Hamlet:** How is that? Have they grown stale from want of practice?

**Rosencrantz:** No, my lord, they are quite as good as ever they were; but they have now to contend with a nest of young boys, little hawks, who speak all their parts in a shrill treble voice, and are most extravagantly applauded for it. These are now all the rage, and they make such a noise on the ordinary stages, as they contemptuously term them, that men carrying swords, fearing to be satirized by these youngsters, are almost afraid to appear.

**Hamlet:** Where do the boys come from, and who supports and pays them? Will they give up acting as soon as their voices break? Or if not, and in time they become ordinary tragedians—as I suppose they will do eventually, unless they find a more profitable means of employment—will they not consider that those who wrote the plays for them did them a great injustice in making them rant against their future profession?

**Rosencrantz:** Well, there have been heated arguments on this point in which both parties have been actively engaged, and the people think it a capital amusement to urge them further. Indeed, at one time, a play was worth nothing whatever unless author and actor diversified the dialogue with references to warfare.

**Hamlet:** Can this be true?

**Guildenstern:** Feeling has raged high on this question, I do assure you.

**Hamlet:** I suppose the youthful players have gained the day.

**Rosencrantz:** O, yes; they not only carry the world with them but the world-bearer as well.

**Hamlet:** There is nothing very remarkable about this after all. The new monarch, my relative, supplies another instance of the way in which fashions change. Many who cared very little for him when he was merely the king's brother, are now willing to pay almost any price for a miniature of him. If science could only discover the cause of this, it would be found, I'll warrant, no unborn trait of human nature.

*[Flourish of trumpets within.]*

**Guildenstern:** Here come the tragedians.

**Hamlet:** Let me tell you again how pleased I am to see you here. Come, shake hands with me. Custom and outward forms are the proper accompaniment of a greeting; allow me to welcome you heartily in this fashion, for fear my condescension to the actors—and I am bound, I must say, at least to appear polite to them—may seem to you a warmer welcome than that which you received. I am, indeed, glad to see you, though my father-in-law and aunt by marriage are mistaken.

**Guildenstern:** How mistaken, your lordship?

**Hamlet:** In thinking me insane. I am only that when the wind is from one point of the compass. At other times I know what I am about.

*[Enter Polonius.]*

**Polonius:** Good day to you, sirs.

**Hamlet:** Listen, Guildenstern; listen, Rosencrantz; listen both of you; that great infant who is speaking to you is still in baby clothes.

40

**Rosencrantz:** He must be in them for the second time then; but they do say that old age is second childhood.

**Hamlet:** I'll wager you he is going to bring us news of the arrival of the actors. Quite true, as you say, it did happen on Monday morning.

**Polonius:** I want to tell you something, your lordship.

**Hamlet:** I want to tell you something, your lordship. At the time when that great Roman tragedian Roscius was—

**Polonius:** The players have arrived, your lordship.

**Hamlet:** Your news is stale, sir.

**Polonius:** But my life—

**Hamlet:** A donkey bore each player in—

**Polonius:** They are brilliant performers, and have never been equalled in any kind of play, romantic, idyllic, tragic, comic or any combination of some or all of these it may please you to choose. It matters not to them whether the Unities are observed or disregarded, and they are equally at home with the serious works of Seneca, or the lively and amusing productions of Plautus. For sticking closely to the book, or improvising when necessary, they are the sort you require.

**Hamlet:** Great Jephthah, ruler of God's people, thou wert indeed blessed—

**Polonius:** In what way, your highness?

**Hamlet:** Well, he had but one child, a lovely maid, upon whom he lavished all his affection.

**Polonius:** [*Aside.*] He is speaking of my child again.

**Hamlet:** Is that no so Jephthah, my friend?

**Polonius:** If you refer to me by that name, your lordship, you are right. I have but one girl, and am devoted to her.

**Hamlet:** That is not the continuation of it.

**Polonius:** Is it not? What is then?

**Hamlet:** "And since divine providence ordained it—" you know the rest—"it so happened as might have been expected." I can say no more of it now, for here come some to shorten my discourse, but the first stanza of the sacred ballad will supply you with the remainder.

[*Enter four or five players.*]

Hearty greetings to you, one and all! It gives me special pleasure to see you in such good health. Kind friends, I rejoice at your coming. Oh, my dear acquaintance! Thou has grown a beard since last we parted; hast thou come to confront me here at home? Gracious, this is surely not my young friend, the heroine! How you have grown! Why, you must be several inches taller than you were at our last meeting. God grant that your voice is not breaking, for then you will be as useless for your occupation as an imperfect coin is unfit for currency. Friends, I am pleased to see you. Come, then, we will begin at once, and, like French sportsmen, we'll not be particular what it is. Give us a sample of your ability; show us what you can do; something with plenty of feeling in it, come now.

**First Player:** Is there any passage you specially prefer, your highness?

**Hamlet:** Well, I was present when you recited something; I don't believe the play was ever performed in its entirety, or, at any rate, on not more than one occasion, for if my memory does not fail me, it did not receive a good reception, being above the comprehension of the ordinary crowd. I, however, considered it, and my opinion was supported by many who were entitled to speak with greater authority than myself, a very superior composition indeed, the scenes following each other in carefully prepared sequence, and the whole thing being put together with propriety as well as dexterity. There was someone, I believe, who complained that the dialogue contained no smart flashes of wit to give piquancy to the plot, and that there was no striving after effect in the style; but, at any rate, it was a straightforward play, with a pure and healthy tone about it, remarkable more for order and proportion than elaborate ornamentation. I was especially fond of one passage in it, the account of his adventures given by Aeneas to the Carthaginian queen, and particularly that part of it in which he describes how the old king of Troy was brutally slain. If you recollect it still, commence at the place where he says—what is it now? O, yes. "That monster, Pyrrhus, tigerish in his fury." It commences thus, does it not? I know it is something about Pyrrhus.

The monster, Pyrrhus, who while concealed in that death-dealing steed, was surpassed in the blackness of his clothing only by the gloom of midnight, and the wickedness of his own savage intentions, has now covered his terrible and swarthy form with a yet more horrid disguise. From top to toe he is entirely enveloped in a coating of red. This ghastly ornamentation consists of human blood, not of Troy's defenders only, but of their children and wives. The heat of the burning buildings has clotted and burnt it into his person, whilst their flames cast a cursed and savage glare over the scene of the tragedy. Consumed thus by flame without and passion within, encrusted with this horrid coating of hardened blood, his eyes flashing like coals of fire, this fiendish monster goes in search of the venerable Priam. Go on from there, will you?

**Polonius:** Bravo, your lordship, well done! Your judgment and expression are alike excellent.

**First Player:** He soon discovers him aiming wild blows at his enemies. His arm is too weak to control his old-fashioned weapon, which remains where it fell, as if unwilling to obey him. Taking him thus at a disadvantage, Pyrrhus falls upon the enfeebled monarch; but so great is his fury that his blow misses its mark. The force with which the cruel weapon falls is so great that even the draft caused by it is sufficient to unman poor Priam and throw him to the ground. The Palace of Troy, which was burning furiously near them, though a thing inanimate, appeared to suffer from the shock, for, with a terrible noise, it tumbled headlong down. The sound arrested Pyrrhus' attention, and his weapon was just about to descend upon the snowy locks of the venerable Priam, remained poised in midair. In this position he continued to stay inactive, like the picture of an oppressor, indifferent alike to his intentions and the object of them. But just as a fierce tempest of thunder, so terrible that it seems to tear the sky asunder, is frequently preceded by an unearthly stillness, the clouds being motionless, not a breath of wind stirring, and everything, in fact, being as silent as the grave, so the inaction of Pyrrhus was but the prelude to a fresh outbreak of his vengeful fury. He rained blows on poor Priam with his bloodstained sword, as pitilessly as if he were one of Vulcan's assistants, engaged in hammering the everlasting mail of the God of War. A curse upon thee, Fortune, false and inconsistent goddess! Ye gods, assemble in full conclave to destroy her sway, crush to pieces the rim and spokes of her wheel, and hurl the remainder headlong from highest bliss to the lowest depth of Hades.

**Polonius:** This speech needs shortening.

**Hamlet:** Well, have it cut when you pay your next visit to the hairdresser. Go on, please, and let me hear about Hecuba.

**First Player:** What a sad sight, too, his muffled wife presented!

**Hamlet:** His muffled wife?

**Polonius:** Muffled wife! That's a fine expression, exceedingly fine.

**First Player:** Her eyes full of blinding tears, her lean and most exhausted frame enveloped only in a covering hastily snatched in her alarm from a bed, a rag upon the stately head that once a crown adorned, she rushed shoeless to and fro, cursing the fury of the fire. It was impossible to gaze upon this spectacle without railing with bitterest taunts against the power of fortune, the author of her afflictions. Verily, if the gods had seen her when she with her own eyes beheld Pyrrhus taking a spiteful pleasure in hacking her husband to pieces, the sudden scream to which she gave vent would have moved the very heavens to tears, and the gods themselves to violent sorrow—that is, if they have any pity at all for mortal woes.

**Polonius:** Why, he has actually turned pale, and is even weeping. I think you had better stop, sir.

**Hamlet:** That will do; on another occasion you may finish it for me. My dear Polonius, see that the entertainers are looked after well. Pay special attention to them now, I say, for it is their duty to summarize and recount the passing events, and it will be more to your advantage to avoid their censure while alive, than to have your tomb storied with your praises after you have gone.

**Polonius:** I shall entertain them, your honor, in a manner befitting their station.

**Hamlet:** Good gracious, sir, that will never do. If everyone were dealt with strictly according to his merits, few indeed would avoid punishment. Entertain them in a manner befitting your nobility of mind and position, and remember that the greater their unworthiness the more admirable is your liberality. Let them go with you.

**Polonius:** Follow me, gentlemen.

**Hamlet:** Go with him, my men, and tomorrow we'll taste your skill. [*Exit Polonius with all the players but the first.*] I wonder, my good fellow, if "The Murder of Gonzago" is on your list of plays.

**First Player:** O, yes, your lordship.

**Hamlet:** Well, that is the play I wish you to perform tomorrow evening, and I suppose that, if necessary, you would be willing to learn and add to it a passage of about sixteen lines, not more, that I shall write out for you.

**First Player:** Certainly, your lordship.

**Hamlet:** That will do then. Go after your friends, but mind you do not make fun of his lordship. [*Exit first player.*] My dear comrades, let me say good-bye to you till later in the evening; we are rejoiced to see you at Elsinore.

**Rosencrantz:** Very well, your highness.

**Hamlet:** Good-bye then, my friends. [*Exit Rosencrantz and Guildenstern.*] By myself, at last! Truly I am a knave, a despicable slave. Is it not an everlasting disgrace to me that this mere actor is able at will to realize an unreal and altogether imaginary grief so vividly that under its influence his face turns pale, moisture dims his eyes, frenzy possesses his looks, sobs choke his utterance, and the entire action of his body conforms with the conception in his mind? And for whose sake? Hecuba's! What special relationship do they bear to each other that her sorrows move him to tears? I wonder how he would behave if the causes that prompt me to express violent grief possessed him. Why, the torrent of his emotion would flood the entire arena, and his dreadful language would hold every member of the audience spellbound, driving the wicked to distraction, terrifying the innocent, perplexing the simple-minded and in fact astounding the sight and hearing of all present.

My behavior, on the other hand, is stupid, irresolute and contemptible. Like a knave or a dreamer, whom nothing will quicken into action, I have not a word to say, not even for a monarch dastardly deprived not only of his rights but of his very existence. I must in sooth be lacking in courage. Were someone to call me a scoundrel, or to insult me by cracking my skull, snatching hair from my face and blowing it back at me, or pulling my nose, or telling me to my face that I lied deeply from my heart, I wonder what I should do!

Heavens! I verily believe I should meekly submit to these indignities, for I must be as devoid of spirit as a dove, and as incapable as that bird of feeling resentment at an injury. If not, long before this, the fowls of the air would have gorged themselves with the foul carrion of this serf, this cruel murderous rascal, this pitiless, traitorous, lascivious and most unnatural monster. Revenge! Revenge! Come, this is mere foolishness. A son who loved his father so well, and who has been specially solicited by supernatural agencies to avenge him, is daring indeed, when all he can do is to rave and swear like a lowborn kitchen wench.

Shame! Shame! Let me set my wits to work. I believe there have been cases where criminals, being present at a tragedy, have been so cut to the heart by the skill with which the piece was acted that they have at once confessed their crimes. So true is it that, however carefully he may conceal his guilt, it will be discovered at last in a most marvellous manner. I'll have a play performed in the presence of the king resembling somewhat the poisoning of my father. I will watch him closely, and probe the very secrets of his heart. Should he only flinch it will be enough.

The apparition may after all be the archfiend himself, for he can adopt any disguise he pleases. What is more likely than that, noticing my frailty and sadness—and it is with natures like mine that he has most power—he is deceiving me in order to get me within his clutches? No, I will wait until I can get some evidence more conclusive. If my uncle's soul is stained with murder, this piece of mine will wring confession from him.

[*Exit.*]

## ACT III · SCENE 1

[*A room in the castle.*]
[*Enter king, queen, Polonius, Ophelia,*
*Rosencrantz and Guildenstern.*]

**King:** Is it not possible, even by a roundabout method, for you to find out the cause of his disorder, which disturbs so dreadfully his peace of mind, and renders him a raving and dangerous madman?

**Rosencrantz:** We did force him to acknowledge that he suffers somewhat from confusion of mind, but we could not get a word from him as to the reason for it.

**Guildenstern:** And he was in no way inclined to be questioned, but with the accustomed skill of those in his condition, cleverly managed to change the conversation whenever we broached the subject of his malady.

**Queen:** What sort of welcome did he give you?

**Rosencrantz:** A most courteous one.

**Guildenstern:** Yet he seemed to have to compel himself to be companionable.

**Rosencrantz:** Slow to open the talk, but ready enough to answer our questions.

**Queen:** Did you try if he was disposed toward any amusement?

**Rosencrantz:** It chanced, your majesty, that as we came hither we overtook a company of actors, and on telling Hamlet of the circumstance he seemed to take great pleasure in the news. They have now arrived, and have already been commanded, I fancy, to give a performance this evening in his presence.

**Polonius:** That is quite so, and he begged me to request his royal parents to make it convenient to attend.

**King:** I will most gladly do so; indeed I am very pleased to learn that they interest him so. Kind sirs, excite him still further to take a greater interest in such pleasures.

**Rosencrantz:** Your highness has said it.

[*Exit Rosencrantz and Guildenstern.*]

**King:** You might also withdraw, dear queen, for we wish Hamlet to meet Ophelia here apparently by chance and have secretly contrived to secure his presence. Polonius and I, who have a perfect right to be spies, intend to place ourselves in such a position that we may see all that happens without his knowing it. In this way we hope to be able

47

to form a candid opinion as to whether or not the malady that affects him is the result of blighted affection.

**Queen:** It shall be as you desire, and I sincerely hope, Ophelia, for your own sake, that it is nothing more dreadful than the power of your charms that has driven him to distraction, for in that case I do not doubt but that your excellent qualities will restore him once more to his own true self, to the advantage of both of you.

**Ophelia:** May it be so, your highness!

*[Exit queen.]*

**Polonius:** Stroll carelessly about, Ophelia. My lord, if such be your desire, let us now be hidden. *[To Ophelia.]* Have this book in your hand, and your appearance of attention to it will be some excuse for your being alone. This is a common fault of ours. Indeed it is a matter of too frequent experience that the most consummate acts of villainy are cloaked under a sanctimonious face and a religious manner.

**King:** *[Aside.]* Unfortunately for me, that is so. How keenly his remark makes me feel the pangs of guilt! The face of the wanton, which owes its loveliness to its artificial covering, is just as hideous in comparison with the cosmetics that adorn it as my actions are in comparison with the plausible speech in which I cloak them. It is grievous, but must be borne.

**Polonius:** To our places, your highness, he is approaching.

*[Exit king and Polonius.]*
*[Enter Hamlet.]*

**Hamlet:** Shall I continue to live or not? This is the momentous decision I am called upon to make. Which is the better part? Patiently to endure the blows and buffetings of a cruel fate or boldly to encounter my innumerable sorrows and vanquish them in the conflict? What is death? Nothing but a deep slumber. And can we assure ourselves that this slumber will ease forever the anguish and the countless inevitable pangs our nature is subject to? This is a conclusion that one might earnestly hope for. Yes, death is indeed a slumber, but what of the visions that may disturb it? This is the drawback. This is what causes us to hesitate before we cast aside the entanglements of our earthly life— the visions that may disturb this final slumber.

Here we find the consideration that causes our afflictions to be so long-lived. Were this not the case, where is the man that would endure the blows and sneers met with in this present life, the injuries inflicted by tyrants, the rudeness of the haughty, the bitter pain of a scorned affection, the tedious slowness of legal proceedings, the incivility of public officials and disdainful rejections that men of worth have calmly to endure at the hands of the worthless, if with a mere dagger he could obtain release from all? Why do we consent to groan and perspire under the heavy burdens of a tedious existence except that a shrinking fear of what is beyond the grave, that unknown land, from the confines of which no wanderer has ever yet come back, perplexes our resolution, causing us to prefer our present evils to those of whose nature we are ignorant?

In this way, speculation on the consequences of our action deprives us of the courage to go through with it, the natural color of our determination becomes tinged with the unhealthy pallor of a careful anxiety, and under this influence, lofty and momentous issues are diverted from their course and become totally inactive. But I must pause, the beautiful Ophelia is present. Fair maid, in thy devotions forget not to ask pardon for my many misdoings.

**Ophelia:** Greetings to your lordship. How has your highness fared during the long period which has elapsed since I saw you last?

**Hamlet:** I have enjoyed perfect health. Pray accept my gratitude for your inquiry.

**Ophelia:** I have here, your honor, some tokens you once gave me, which I have for some time desired to return. Will you kindly take them back?

**Hamlet:** I cannot, for I have given nothing to you.

**Ophelia:** Most gracious lord, you did give them, as you are perfectly aware, and they have been very precious to me, for the endearing expressions which accompanied them. Now that you have no kind words for me please receive them back, for to a person of any dignity of character, costly presents lose all their value when the donors of them cease to be affectionate. Here they are, your lordship.

**Hamlet:** How's this? Have you grown virtuous?

**Ophelia:** What do you mean?

**Hamlet:** Are you not beautiful?

**Ophelia:** Why do you ask, my lord?

**Hamlet:** If you are virtuous and beautiful, your virtue should allow no one, not even itself, to have intercourse with your beauty.

**Ophelia:** What better companion could beauty have, your lordship, than virtue?

**Hamlet:** A much better one. It is much more common for a virtuous nature to be degraded by the influence of a lovely form, than it is for a fair, though corrupt, person to be uplifted by association with a noble and upright one. Formerly, people considered this a strange notion, but it has frequently of late been shown to be true. There was a time when I was fond of you.

**Ophelia:** So I certainly supposed, your honor, from your conduct.

**Hamlet:** You were foolish to put any trust in me. The original depravity of our sinful nature is bound to leave its trait whatever moral excellences we may ingraft into it. I never cared anything for you.

**Ophelia:** So much the greater then was my error.

**Hamlet:** Go and embrace the holy vows of a nun. The world will be all the purer without our offspring. Judged by this world's standard I am fairly honorable, yet I could make confession of deeds so vile that it would be an advantage to me never to have existed. Self-esteem, vindictiveness and lust for power are among my failings, and the sins that are ever ready at my call surpass the bounds of conception. I have neither inventiveness to plan them, nor is life long enough to put them into practice. Why are such wretched creatures as I allowed to creep about the face of this planet? We are downright rogues, every one of us, and should not be trusted. Away now, seek refuge in a convent. Your sire, is he here?

**Ophelia:** No, your lordship, he is in his own house.

**Hamlet:** Lock him up there then, so that his folly may be confined to his own dwelling. Good-bye.

**Ophelia:** Ye Powers on high, assist him in his affliction.

**Hamlet:** If, in spite of me, you persist in becoming a wife, I prophesy this trouble as your marriage portion; though you be perfect in your chastity, the finger of scorn will still be pointed at you. Be advised now: take the veil. Good-bye. Stay, if it is decreed that you must wed, choose a simpleton for your mate, for men of sense know how your unfaithfulness disfigures them. Seek a convent then, and that speedily. Good-bye.

**Ophelia:** Merciful heavens! Bring him again to his right mind.

**Hamlet:** I know very well how you women behave. Not content with the complexion that Nature has bestowed upon you, you rouge and powder it and endeavor to change it. You dance lewd dances, you walk with a mincing gait, you speak childishly, you immodestly misname the things that God has created and pretend that you do it because you know no better. Begone! I am determined to put up with no more of such behavior. It has driven me from my senses. We will have done with weddings altogether for the future. The wedded ones, with a single exception, shall continue in that state, but the remainder shall remain single. Haste then to a convent.

*[Exit.]*

**Ophelia:** O, the piteous spectacle presented by the downfall of this splendid intellect! Here we see one fitted to grace the royal presence, endowed with the eloquence of a man of learning and the skill in arms of a warrior, utterly deprived of his reason. The chief hope and ornament of the State that he so well adorned, the pattern of good taste in dress, the model of excellence in figure, and the one looked up to by all as an example to be copied, is now laid low. Truly I, who so eagerly drank the sweet words of his solemn promises, am now the most dispirited and miserable of my sex, for I behold the elements that produce such perfect harmony in that superb and kingly nature at war with each other, like bells naturally melodious in tone sounded in jarring discord. I see a youth in the full bloom of his early manhood, incomparably beautiful, both in figure and face, blighted with insanity. O miserable me, that I should have lived to witness such a change in one I loved so well!

*[Re-enter king and Polonius.]*

**King:** Well, I am quite sure that he cherishes no tenderness of feeling for your daughter, and though his language was rather incoherent, it was not the speech of a lunatic. He has something on his mind which he has anxiously pondered over until his spirits have become depressed, and I am afraid that the result will be some calamity. I intend, therefore, to take prompt and decisive measures to anticipate this. I will send him off to England to claim the revenue due to us, which is still unpaid. It may be that the various sights he will see on his voyage, and in the foreign lands he visits, will drive away this grief that has somewhat taken possession of his feelings, and over which his continual brooding has changed him from his usual state. What is your opinion about the matter?

**Polonius:** I entirely approve of your plan. Nevertheless, I am still inclined to think that his unrequited passion for my daughter was the primary cause of his malady. Well, Ophelia, it is no use recounting what has passed between yourself and Prince Hamlet, for every word was audible to us.

Adopt whatever plan you think proper, your highness, but if you can see your way to agree to it, I advise you to make arrangements for his royal mother to see him alone when the players have finished, and try to get him to tell her the cause of his sorrow. Tell her to question him quite plainly, and I'll hide myself so that I can hear all that passes. If the interview be fruitless, let him be dispatched to England, or restrained in whatever other place seems best to your judgment.

**King:** I shall certainly do as you suggest, for we cannot allow the insanity of a person of his rank to remain without supervision.

*[Exit.]*

## ACT III · SCENE 2

*[A hall in the castle.]*
*[Enter Hamlet and players.]*

**Hamlet:** Deliver the passage, I beg, in an easy natural manner, just as I recited it to you. Do not utter it in a loud ranting tone as many members of your profession do, or I might as well engage the bellman to deliver it. Be not too free with your gestures and do not move your arms about in this fashion, but restrain yourself, for even when your emotion is most intense and at its very summit, it is your duty to learn to use a certain amount of moderation in order to make it flow gently onward. Nothing wounds my feelings more deeply than to see some sturdy player in a wig spoiling, absolutely ruining in fact, the expression of a strongly emotional passage in order to gain applause from a rough crowd on the floor of the house, who, as a rule, can appreciate nothing but pantomimic gestures and bombast. Why, a worthless player like that, who surpasses Termagant himself in violence, deserves punishing and would be punished too, if I had my way. Even Herod could not rage more. Don't do it, please.

**First Player:** Have no fear on that account, my lord.

**Hamlet:** Do not, however, fall into the opposite error of being too spiritless, but be guided by common sense. Let your speech and gesture quite accord with each other, always bearing this special point in mind, never to go beyond the limits of natural moderation. Anything in excess of that is opposed to the objects of stage representation, the aim of which has been from the very first inception of the theater, to this present time, to portray things as they really are, representing morally excellent personages as worthy of admiration and morally despicable ones as deserving of contempt, and giving, in fact, a perfect picture in appearance and character of the period represented. By overacting or too feebly representing a part, the player may succeed in amusing the ignorant, but at the same time he deeply offends those who are really capable of judging, and the opinion of one of these latter ought to have more value in your estimation than a household of the former.

I have myself witnessed actors and heard people commend them too, who—and I have no intention of being irreverent—being unable to speak like Christians or to carry themselves like any men whatever, Christian or heathen, have stalked pompously about the stage, roaring so loudly, that they made one think that they were not human beings at all, but that some bungling day laborers had tried their hands at making men and had failed most miserably, so wretched was their copy of our nature.

**First Player:** I think you will find, my lord, that we have fairly well got rid of that sort of thing.

**Hamlet:** You should abolish it entirely. Moreover, you ought to make those who take the part of the fool stick closely to the lines, and not bring in anything of their own. Some of them, I know, begin laughing themselves, merely to get some of the more empty-headed members of the audience to join in with them, even if by so doing they may cause people to miss some vital point in connection with the plot. This is sorry conduct, and proves that the clown who is guilty of it has most despicable ideals. Make your preparations at once.

*[Exit players.]*

*[Enter Polonius, Rosencrantz and Guildenstern.]*

Well, your lordship, is his majesty willing to see this play?

**Polonius:** Yes, he and the queen would like to see it at once.

**Hamlet:** Tell the performers then, to be as quick as possible. *[Exit Polonius.]* You also would oblige me by assisting him in hurrying them up.

**Rosencrantz:** ⎱ With pleasure, your highness.
**Guildenstern:** ⎰

*[Exit Rosencrantz and Guildenstern.]*

**Hamlet:** I say, Horatio!

*[Enter Horatio.]*

**Horatio:** Here I am, my dear master, ready to do whatever you bid me.

**Hamlet:** In all my dealings with men, Horatio, I have never met one more honorable than thyself.

**Horatio:** My gracious prince—

**Hamlet:** O, I do not say this to please your vanity, for in what way would my fortunes be advanced by so doing, seeing that the whole sum of wealth upon which your maintenance depends consists of your inexhaustible fund of good humor? Nothing is to be gained by using honeyed words to people without means, so I advise all who would be flatterers to keep them for those who are foolishly ostentatious, and to bend their ready knees when some profit may be gained by their adulation. Listen to me then. From the first moment when my inmost heart was free to make a selection among men, and was capable of making it wisely, I have centered my affections entirely upon you. Though you have met with many sorrows, you have always seemed unconscious of their presence, accepting the good and evil chances of life with the same philosophic calm.

Happy, indeed, are they who are endowed with that just

mixture of passion and reasoning that renders them incapable of being made the sport and plaything of every idle chance. Such men as you, Horatio, who are entirely masters of their emotions, are the men upon whom I delight to lavish the utmost bounds of my affection. But I am speaking too freely upon this subject. A dramatic performance takes place in his majesty's presence this evening, and it contains an incident closely resembling that whereby, as I mentioned, my parent lost his life.

Now, I wish you, during the progress of this part of the play, to focus your utmost powers of observation upon the king. If one passage in it fails to make him betray his carefully concealed wickedness, I have been deceived by some accursed spirit, and have wronged my uncle with suppositions as black at Etna's smoke. Notice him very carefully, because I am going to fix my gaze steadily upon his countenance. When the play is over, we will compare our opinions with regard to his appearance.

**Horatio:** Depend upon it, your lordship. If a single guilty look of his escapes my notice, I am willing to suffer suitable punishment for my carelessness.

**Hamlet:** Their majesties are approaching, so I had better behave frivolously. Secure a good position now.

[*Danish march. A flourish of trumpets. Enter king, queen, Polonius, Ophelia, Rosencrantz, Guildenstern and other lords attendant, with the guard carrying torches.*]

**King:** Hamlet, my dear kinsman, how are you?

**Hamlet:** In truth, I fare exceedingly well on the same food as the chameleon, that is, air heavily charged, in my case, with expectations. It is a diet, however, that would not do to fatten fowls.

**King:** I cannot accept this, Hamlet, as a reply to my question, for it has no connection with it.

**Hamlet:** No more can I. [*To Polonius.*] You told me, sir, that you went in for acting in your college days.

**Polonius:** That is quite true, your highness, and my performances were thought a great deal of.

**Hamlet:** What part did you take?

**Polonius:** I played Julius Caesar and was slain in the Capitol by Brutus.

**Hamlet:** He was indeed a brute to slay a capital fellow like you in such a place. Is it not time the performance was beginning?

**Rosencrantz:** Yes, your honor, the actors are only awaiting your permission to commence.

**Queen:** Hamlet, my son, take a seat by your mother.

**Hamlet:** I cannot, mother dear. This more powerful magnet retains me.

**Polonius:** [*To the king.*] Did you hear what he said, your majesty?

**Ophelia:** Your highness is mirthful.

**Hamlet:** Do you refer to me?

**Ophelia:** Certainly, your highness.

**Hamlet:** Heavens! It merely serves as an excuse for the composition of silly verses. How can I be otherwise than joyful? Don't you see how my mother is enjoying herself two short hours after her husband's funeral?

**Ophelia:** Your highness must know that it is now four months since his death.

**Hamlet:** Well, if so much time as that has elapsed, those who please may go into mourning, I shall wear a suit of rich magnificence. Think of it, so long dead and his memory still green. Why, if such be the case, a celebrity need not despair of being remembered even for six months after his demise. Yet I am afraid he will have to erect some conspicuous memorial of himself or he will soon sink into oblivion like the once renowned hobbyhorse which, as a popular ballad has it, is now quite forgotten.

[*Oboes play. The show enters.*]

[*Enter a king and a queen very lovingly; the queen embracing him and he her. She kneels, and makes show of protestation to him. He takes her up, and declines his head upon her neck; lays him down upon a bank of flowers: she, seeing him asleep, leaves him. Soon comes a fellow, who takes his crown, kisses it, and pours poison in the king's ears, and exits. The queen returns, finds the king dead, and makes passionate commotion. The poisoner, with some two or three mutes, comes in again, seemingly to lament with her. The dead body is carried away. The poisoner courts the queen with gifts: she seems unpersuaded for a short time, but in the end accepts his love.*]

**Ophelia:** What does this signify, your lordship?

**Hamlet:** This, my lady, is a piece of insidious knavery and it signifies trouble.

**Ophelia:** Probably it is intended to give us some idea of the plot.

[*Enter Prologue.*]

**Hamlet:** Well, you will be informed directly. This man, I suppose, is going to reveal everything. It's a way these actors have.

**Prologue:** We submit our play to your kind judgment and crave a respectful attention for ourselves and it.

**Hamlet:** What is this, an introduction to the play, or a motto for a ring?

**Ophelia:** It certainly did not last long, your lordship.

**Hamlet:** As long as feminine affection.

[*Enter two players, king and queen.*]

**Player King:** The chariot of the sun god has made thirty complete revolutions of the briny world of waters and the curved surface of the land, and the moon has made just twelve times this number of journeys round the earth, waxing and waning as she beamed upon her with reflected rays, since the tender regard for each other which made us one was sealed by the formal union of ourselves in the holy bonds of matrimony.

**Player Queen:** May the motions of the same heavenly orbs compel us to confess that a similar period has elapsed before the flame of our affections is extinguished. Yet, alas, you have been so poorly for some time now, so melancholy and unlike your usual self that I am anxious about you. Do not, however, allow my anxiety in any way to cause you any uneasiness, your lordship, for feminine anxiety and regard are always disproportionate to the object—either not existing at all or being much in excess of what they ought to be. You have already experienced the full extent of my affection for you, so you are in a position to measure the anxiety I feel, for they rise and fall together. An all-absorbing affection magnifies the most trifling uncertainties into objects of anxious dread, and conversely, the exaggeration of light suspicions into great ones, is the true mark of a tender affection.

**Player King:** In truth, dearest, I am afraid that I am not destined to enjoy your society much longer; my vital energies are ceasing to perform their proper work. You, however, shall continue to inhabit this beautiful earth respected and adored, and it may chance that on some future occasion some other man, quite as loving as myself, may claim you for his bride.

**Player Queen:** Speak no more, I beg, for very shame. 'Twould be an act of basest disloyalty even to harbor such a thought. If ever I marry again, may it be to a life of utter misey. Only those who have destroyed their first lord ever marry another.

**Hamlet:** [*Aside.*] How bitter are her words, judged by her future conduct!

**Player Queen:** The inducements that lead people to embrace matrimony more than once are mean considerations of gain, never of affection; and I will be doubly dyed with the guilt of murder before I submit to the fond caresses of a second mate.

**Player King:** I am quite convinced of your sincerity in making these protestations, but it is a matter of everyday occurrence to see resolutions broken. They exist only so long as they are remembered, and, though very robust at their inception, soon lose all the strength they ever possessed. They are not unlike fruit in this respect, which is at first firmly fixed to the tree, but on reaching maturity, drops of its own accord. It is only right that we should be allowed to break our resolutions at will, for they are duties we owe to ourselves alone. Besides, they are generally made at some moment of deep feeling, and when the feeling has passed away, the resolution is found to have passed with it. This is the invariable fate of all actions proposed in some moment of intense sorrow or delight. They last no longer than the passion which conceived them.

The same temperament that is most liable to be depressed with sorrow is also most prone to be elevated with delight, and the slightest provocation is sufficient to cause it to pass from the one extreme to the other. All things, even the earth itself, are liable to change and decay, so we can scarcely be surprised if the affection that others have for ourselves should depend upon our worldly prosperity. And, indeed, it is a matter that still remains to be settled, which influence is the stronger, that of affection upon material prosperity, or material prosperity upon affection. Notice the haste with which the crowd of parasites deserts the fallen patron, and the change that comes over the former foes of the unexpectedly rich.

And so it has ever been, affection is the handmaid of prosperity, and friends are always most abundant to those who need them least. Let some one, however, who really needs a friend, endeavor to make use of one of these insincere ones, and he will immediately discover the hidden ill will with which the latter regards him. So, to come back in due sequence to the point from which I started, what we resolve, and what we are destined to do, are so directly opposed to each other, that we are constantly seeing our plans upset. We are at liberty to propose, but the disposal rests in other hands than ours. Just now you are persuaded you will never marry again, but my death would entirely change your point of view.

**Player Queen:** May the ground cease to supply me with nourishment, and the celestial bodies withhold their bright beams; may my days be without pleasure, and my nights without sleep; may all my fondest wishes and expectations result in black despair; may the utmost aim of my life be the cell and meager fare of the hermit; may every obstacle from which happiness shrinks back with fear, encounter everything to which I wish success and overthrow it; may continuous contention be my lot both in this world and the world to come, if I should ever marry a second time!

**Hamlet:** How dreadful if she should prove unfaithful in spite of all this!

**Player King:** You have made most solemn protestations. Withdraw, my love, for a short time. I feel very weary and would like to pass in slumber some hours of this tiresome day.

[*Sleeps.*]

**Player Queen:** May slumber soothe thy mind and nothing ever happen to estrange us from each other!

**Hamlet:** Well, mother, what do you think about the piece?

**Queen:** I am afraid she is much too free with her solemn declarations of loyalty.

**Hamlet:** She will be true to them, however.

**King:** Are you familiar with the plot of this piece? I hope it contains nothing objectionable.

**Hamlet:** Nothing at all, my lord; everything is in fun, the poisoning and all. There is nothing in the least objectionable, I assure you.

**King:** What is the name of the piece?

**Hamlet:** It is called "Mousetrap," and the name is a figurative one. It gives an exact representation of a crime that took place in Vienna. The king is called Gonzago, and his queen, Baptista. You will be able to judge for yourself soon what a dastardly act it was. That is nothing, however, to your highness, and people like ourselves who have clear consciences. It does not affect us—let those who feel the consciousness of guilt be offended by the play. Our susceptibilities are unwounded.

*[Enter Lucianus.]*

This man's name is Lucianus. Gonzago is his uncle.

**Ophelia:** No interpreter is needed while you are present, my lord.

**Hamlet:** O, if it comes to that, I would be an excellent one to explain the movements of the figures at a marionette show where the dolls represented you and your fiancé.

**Ophelia:** Your answer is richer in wit, but poorer in decorum than I could wish it to be.

**Hamlet:** That is how you ladies hold your partners in marriage. Now, villain, stop making such horrible grimaces and get to work. The screeching raven cries out loud for retribution.

**Lucianus:** Villainous intention, nimble fingers, and a suitable potion; an opportune moment which seems to have conspired with me to assist my plan; not a soul in sight to observe my action. Foul concoction of herbs gathered in darkness, blighted and corrupted by Hecate's threefold curse, let thy innate witchcraft and deadly qualities instantly dispossess the healthy vitality of this sleeper.

*[Pours the poison into the sleeper's ear.]*

**Hamlet:** He takes his life by means of this drug as he thus sleeps, in order to obtain the kingship. The king is one Gonzago, and an account of the murder in exquisite Italian still exists. If you wait a few moments, you will witness the crafty arts by which this villain persuades his victim's wife to marry him.

**Ophelia:** His majesty is on his feet.

**Hamlet:** Not alarmed, surely, by a mere fictitious crime.

**Queen:** What ails your highness?

**Polonius:** Bid the performance cease.

**King:** Kindle the lamps at once.

**All:** The lamps, the lamps!

*[Exit all but Hamlet and Horatio.]*

**Hamlet:** What if the wounded stag retires to shed tears of grief in solitude whilst her lord frisks about unharmed? Was it not ever thus? If some are to slumber, others must keep awake. Now supposing all other means of earning a livelihood failed me, could I not by means of this, together with an appropriate costume, feather trimmings, and huge rosettes in my slashed shoes, obtain for me a partnership in a company of actors?

**Horatio:** They might obtain part of one.

**Hamlet:** Part of one would not do for me. For, my good friend, I wish to tell you that this kingdom has been forcibly deprived of its ruler—a paragon among kings, and his place is now occupied by a downright popinjay.

**Horatio:** Why did you not finish it properly?

**Hamlet:** Horatio, my friend, I am willing to stake almost anything on the truth of what the apparition told me. Did you not notice the king?

**Horatio:** I did, indeed, your highness.

**Hamlet:** While Lucianus was delivering his speech?

**Horatio:** I specially noticed him then.

**Hamlet:** That is capital, we will have a tune now—bring in the instruments. If his majesty does not care for the play, well, then he doesn't care for it; that is all. Here, let us have a tune!

*[Re-enter Rosencrantz and Guildenstern.]*

**Guildenstern:** Will your highness deign to converse with me for a few moments?

**Hamlet:** As long as you please, my friend.

**Guildenstern:** My lord, his majesty—

**Hamlet:** Well, is there anything wrong with him?

**Guildenstern:** Has withdrawn to his apartments very much upset.

**Hamlet:** Has he been drinking too freely?

**Guildenstern:** No, your highness, on the other hand, it is anger that troubles him.

**Hamlet:** It would be much wiser on your part to report this to a medical man, than to me. I am afraid if I were called upon to treat him, it would but increase his malady.

**Guildenstern:** I should be glad if your highness would put your remarks into some sensible form and not rush so madly from the topic of our conversation.

**Hamlet:** I am all attention; say on.

**Guildenstern:** I come to you at the request of your royal mother, who is at present enduring the greatest mental distress.

**Hamlet:** Your presence, then, is most acceptable.

**Guildenstern:** On the contrary, my lord, the manner of your welcome is not of the kind that would lead one to think so. If you will be good enough to give me a reasonable reply, I will deliver the queen's message. Failing that, I beg to close the interview by asking your permission to go back to your mother.

**Hamlet:** I am sorry I am unable to oblige you.

**Guildenstern:** In what way, your highness?

**Hamlet:** By giving you a reasonable reply; my mind is deranged. Still, I shall gladly give you, or I should say, the queen, the best reply that is in my power. So without further delay, let us get to business. You were saying that the queen—

**Rosencrantz:** Well, her majesty has told us that she is filled with the greatest surprise and wonder at your conduct.

**Hamlet:** I must indeed be a remarkable child, to cause my mother such surprise. But surely this is not the whole message. You must have more to tell me than my mother's surprise. Proceed.

**Rosencrantz:** She would like to have a few words with you in her chamber before you retire for the night.

**Hamlet:** If she were tenfold more related to me than she is, I would not refuse her this. Is there any other business you would like to transact with me?

**Rosencrantz:** We used to be good friends, your highness.

**Hamlet:** For my part we are yet. I call these hands to witness it.

**Rosencrantz:** Tell us, then, your highness, what has deranged you. You must know that you are closing up the only way of escape from your sorrows, by refusing to share them with one who loves you.

**Hamlet:** Well, my friend, my prospects of promotion are but scanty.

**Rosencrantz:** Surely you are making a mistake, seeing that the reigning monarch has already recommended you as his successor.

**Hamlet:** True, true, my friend, but remember the old and rather trite saying: What is the poor horse going to do while his fodder is being cultivated?

[*Re-enter players with flutes.*]

Here come the musical instruments! Hand me one! Step aside with me for a moment. What is the reason for these subterfuges by which you try to force some confession from me, which I am unwilling to make?

**Guildenstern:** Excuse me, your highness, it is the daring nature of the task I am in honor bound to perform that makes me act less respectfully toward you than my affection warrants.

**Hamlet:** I don't quite grasp your meaning. Let me hear you play a tune upon this flute.

**Guildenstern:** I do not play it, your highness.

**Hamlet:** Let me urge you.

**Guildenstern:** Really, I am unable.

**Hamlet:** Come now, as a personal favor to myself.

**Guildenstern:** I cannot play a single note, your highness.

**Hamlet:** Nothing could possibly be simpler. You have merely to cover these holes with your fingers and thumb, place it to your lips and blow, then it will give forth the most charming melody. See, these are the places where the fingers are to be placed.

**Guildenstern:** But I have not the necessary power over them to make them give forth harmonious sounds. I lack the dexterity.

**Hamlet:** Then you must indeed consider me a wretched being. You wish to have such a command over me, as to make me speak whenever and whatever you please, and you assume that you have already got it. You would like to extort from me the inmost secrets of my heart, and make me give utterance to my every thought. Yes, my vocal chords, tiny as they are, could utter many things that you long to hear, had you only the power to make them. Good heavens, sir! I am less difficult to manipulate than a mere flute? Regard me as what you please—you may be able to annoy me, but you shall not impose upon me.

[Enter Polonius.]

**Polonius:** Your mother wishes to say something to you at once, your highness.

**Hamlet:** Look at that cloud, which in form bears a striking resemblance to a camel.

**Polonius:** Truly, its appearance is remarkably like that animal.

**Hamlet:** I believe now its form reminds me of a weasel.

**Polonius:** Well, its shape certainly suggests the back of a weasel.

**Hamlet:** Perhaps I should compare it to a whale.

**Polonius:** A very just comparison, too.

**Hamlet:** Very well, tell her majesty I will be with her immediately. [*Aside.*] So great is their desire to humor me that they comply with any statement of mine, however ridiculous it may be. Tell her to expect me immediately.

**Polonius:** She shall have your message.

[Exit Polonius.]

**Hamlet:** That promise is not hard to keep. I would be alone, kind sirs.

[Exit all but Hamlet.]

This is precisely that hour of darkness when witchcraft doth most abound, when the spirits of the dead roam abroad and the very air seems to be tainted with the poisonous vapors of the lower world. I, too, am affected with its influence. I feel as if I could wallow in living blood and do deeds so cruel and murderous that one would shudder to behold them in open daylight. Let me pause, however, until my interview with the queen is over. While there, may I never forget that she is my mother. May I never, though fully resolved that the guilty must suffer, entertain for a single moment the thought of matricide. I shall be brutally candid to her without degrading myself; my words will pierce her like sharp swords, but I shall employ no other weapons. They will, in fact, misrepresent my intentions to this extent that, no matter how severely they may sting her, nothing will induce me to confirm them by action.

### ACT III · SCENE 3
[*A room in the castle.*]
[*Enter king, Rosencrantz and Guildenstern.*]

**King:** I am inclined to take a rather serious view of his malady, and consider that it would be very dangerous to allow him, while in this state, to roam about unchecked. Accordingly, I have decided to send him to England in your company; so make the necessary preparations for your voyage and I shall at once prepare the authoritative letter you will take with you. The conditions upon which our safety depends cannot tolerate the risks that constantly arise from his fits of insanity and threaten our very person.

**Guildenstern:** Our preparations shall be made. The welfare of the numberless subordinates that depend entirely upon your royal highness is a duty that is sacred and binding upon you.

**Rosencrantz:** Even a private individual is under an obligation to defend himself from injury by every means that his ingenuity can contrive; how infinitely greater then, is the obligation in the case of one with whose welfare the very existence of hundreds of others is bound up. The death of a king is not a single calamity, but, like a whirlpool which swallows up all neighboring objects, it involves the destruction of everything connected with him. It may be compared to some huge wheel poised on the topmost crag of a great elevation and having attached to it, firmly and loosely, many other smaller objects. When this begins to roll headlong down, everything that is fastened to it or in any way connected with it, however trifling, shares in its violent overthrow. So it is, the smallest grief felt by the king is sufficient to plunge the whole land into general mourning.

**King:** Prepare yourselves at once then, I beg, for the journey you must undertake so soon, for we must take some measures to restrain this danger which at present has too much liberty.

**Rosencrantz:** } We will be ready as soon as possible.
**Guildenstern:** }

*[Exit Rosencrantz and Guildenstern.]*
*[Enter Polonius.]*

**Polonius:** He is now on the way, your highness, to see the queen in her chamber, and I intend to be stationed behind the hangings in order that I may overhear what is said. She is sure to administer a sound reproof to him, but as you in your wisdom remarked, it is better that someone else should be in a favorable position to furnish a report of the interview besides his mother, who would naturally be prone to side with her offspring. Good-bye, my lord, I shall let you have, before you retire for the night, a full account of all that has passed between them.

**King:** I am much obliged to you, my good friend.

[*Exit Polonius.*]

How loathsome in God's sight is the foul crime of which I am guilty! It is branded with the first and earliest of all curses—the curse of Cain. Prompted as I am by desire and determination to crave forgiveness, I am still unable to do so. Powerful though my purpose may be, my crime is even more powerful and subdues it. Thus I remain inactive, doubtfully hesitating at what point to commence, like one upon whom have been imposed two contrary and conflicting duties. Even though I were blasted and befouled by the murder of many brothers, may I not rely upon the mercy of a gracious God to purify me from every guilty stain?

What is the purpose of divine grace, except directly to oppose and drive away sin? Do we not pray either to be prevented from falling into sin, or, having fallen, to be forgiven? Seeing that such is the case, why then need I be cast down? My offence is done with. Yet how shall I frame a condition to suit my case? I cannot crave pardon for my vile deed while I retain the very things for which it was committed—the kingship, the realization of my hopes, and my wife. Surely it is not possible to be forgiven and at the same time continue to hold the advantages gained by the crime. Upon this morally depraved earth of ours it is possible by the aid of gold for an offender to avoid entirely the just penalty of his crime. Indeed, it not infrequently happens that the bribe he tenders to the officers of the law is the very wealth that has been so wickedly acquired.

In heaven, however, matters are different. There can be no evasion there. Not only does the offence appear in its true colors, but the perpetrators are forced to give the most damning testimony against themselves. If that is so then, what remains for me to do but to test the efficacy of contrition and find out what it is and is not capable of doing. It is surely useless, however, if unaccompanied by any amendment of life. Alas, then, for the utter misery of my plight, for the wickedness of my sin-stained heart, for my entangled spirit, making frantic efforts to escape from its difficulties and becoming more entangled with every effort! Assist me, O ye powers of heaven! Hasten to save me! Though unwilling, let me bend myself in supplication. Let my spirit, so unyielding by nature, become as pliant as that of an infant of tender years. Forgiveness may still be mine.

[*Retires and kneels.*]
[*Enter Hamlet.*]

**Hamlet:** Here is my opportunity for immediate revenge while he is engaged in prayer. I'll take advantage of it and hurry him off at once to be with the angels. Would this, however, be vengeance? The matter is one for careful consideration. Here is a cowardly wretch who has murdered my father, and to requite him for it, I, upon whom the duty of revenge has naturally fallen, become the means whereby he is dispatched to eternal bliss. Why, this is conferring the greatest possible benefit upon him instead of wreaking vengeance. My parent was slain in the very midst of a worldy and sensuous life, when his sins were most numerous and in their full prime and vigor. How it will fare with him at the Throne of Grace none but his Maker can tell, but as far as we are capable of judging from a human standpoint, he will fare badly indeed. Could I then be said to have avenged his death if I killed his murderer while cleansing his heart from guilt, and fully prepared and ready to meet his end? Most assuredly not.

Back to your sheath, then, my sword, and wait until I can grasp thee upon a more terrible occasion. Let me find him stupefied with drink, in a storm of passion or in some wicked act of carnal indulgence. Let me find him gambling, cursing, or engaged in some other occupation that has no connection whatever with his spiritual health. That will be the time to give him such a fall that, fleeing from heaven, he may hurry downward to the place for which the vileness of his sins so eminently befits him. The queen is waiting for me. This temporary forbearance of mine is like a medicine which only delays the fatal end of the disease.

*[Exit Hamlet.]*

**King:** My lips utter the prayers, but my heart is not with the words I utter. Such petitions as these, which are not the outcome of true penitence, God never deigns to hear.

*[Exit king.]*

## ACT III · SCENE 4

*[The queen's chamber.]*
*[Enter queen and Polonius.]*

**Polonius:** Your son will be here directly. See that you are severe with him. Give him to understand that his escapades are becoming so unrestrained that they are no longer tolerable, and that your majesty has had to interfere, on more than one occasion, to save him from the anger that would otherwise have fallen upon him. I will conceal myself just at this spot. Do not forget to speak to him in the plainest possible language.

**Hamlet:** *[Within.]* Are you there, mother?

**Queen:** Do not be afraid; you may depend upon my doing exactly as you wish. Step aside now, for he is approaching.

*[Polonius hides behind the tapestry.]*
*[Enter Hamlet.]*

**Hamlet:** Well, mother, why have you sent for me?

**Queen:** Your behavior, my son, has caused your father exceeding displeasure.

**Hamlet:** Your behavior, mother, has caused my father exceeding displeasure.

**Queen:** That will do now. I am afraid that you are speaking frivolously.

**Hamlet:** And I am afraid, mother, that you are speaking sinfully.

**Queen:** Hamlet, what do you mean by speaking to me in such language?

**Hamlet:** Why, what have I said?

**Queen:** You are surely not aware to whom you are speaking.

**Hamlet:** I am perfectly aware. I can swear to that effect. I am speaking to the noblest lady in all the land, the consort of her own brother-in-law, and to my sorrow, I confess, my parent.

**Queen:** If this is the way you are going to speak, I had better bring someone who will force you to use more moderate language.

**Hamlet:** Take your seat again, mother, and do not stir. I intend to keep you there until I reveal to you, as in a mirror, the true condition of your heart.

**Queen:** What do you mean? Do you intend to murder me? Save me! Save me!

**Polonius:** [*Behind.*] Here, I say, assistance! Assistance! Hello!

**Hamlet:** [*Drawing his sword.*] What have we here, a spy? Then I'll wager a small sum I kill him outright.

[*Stabs his sword through the tapestry.*]

**Polonius:** [*Behind.*] Heavens! He has killed me.

[*Falls and dies.*]

**Queen:** Alas! Have you slain him?

**Hamlet:** I have no idea. Was my uncle concealed there?

**Queen:** Ah, me! This is a reckless and cruel act.

**Hamlet:** A cruel act! But not quite as wicked as that of murdering a monarch, and then wedding his brother.

**Queen:** Murdering a monarch?

**Hamlet:** Yes, mother, that is what I said.

[*He lifts up the tapestry and discovers Polonius.*]
Well, headstrong wretch, this is the end of your stupid intrusions. I thought it was your master I was striking. Accept the fate to which your conduct has led you. You see that even to meddle in the affairs of other people is a business filled with some risk. Cease making these outward demonstrations of grief. Remain quietly in your seat, and let me make you feel true sorrow. For it is my intention to do so if such a thing is possible, if your heart has not become so casehardened by pernicious habit, that it forms an impenetrable barrier against all feeling.

**Queen:** Tell me the offence which causes you to attack me with such clamorous incivility.

**Hamlet:** You have done a deed which dims the luster of all that adorns chastity, and commends it to favor; which degrades purity into a mere pretence; which removes the charm that adorns the brow of a pure affection, and replaces it by a shameless flush; which causes the solemn promises of matrimony to be of no more worth than those of a confirmed gambler. An act, in fact, which takes away from the marriage ceremony its very essence, and leaves the holy service nothing but an extravagant jingle of meaningless phrases. The sky assumes a vehement aspect, and even this firm planet of ours, with saddened countenance, as though the judgment were at hand, is depressed with anxiety at the sight of such a deed.

**Queen:** Alas, what deed of mine merits such a harsh and stormy introduction?

**Hamlet:** Compare the two portraits that are before you; they are lifelike representations of two brothers. Notice the nobility stamped on the forehead of this one—the waving hair of Apollo, the brow of Jupiter, the awe-inspiring and imperious look of Mars, the posture of Mercury the Messenger, at the moment of his descent upon the summit of some lofty mount. A figure, in short, comprising so many excellences, that it seemed as if every deity had stamped him with some mark of approval, so that all might know that this was the pinnacle of human perfection. Such a man was your former consort. Behold the other picture now, that of your present one, whose very presence seems to bring infection with it, as a diseased ear of wheat blights its healthy neighbor.

Your perception of beauty is surely deficient, else how could you have ceased to draw your sustenance from this noble and refined source, in order to glut yourself upon this gross and sensual one? Have you any perception of beauty at all? Ardent affection could not possibly have misled you, for at your time of life the blood ceases to burn with passion, its fire is subdued, and love's choice obeys the dictates of reason. What reasonable being, however, could make such a change? You cannot be devoid of feeling: your emotion proves it; but your feelings must surely be diseased, for even an insane person would not make such a mistake, nor is sensibility ever so completely under the power of insane delusions, but that it retains some power of selection, however small, to aid decision when one object is so much superior to the other.

Some evil spirit most assuredly has blindfolded and cheated you. The sense of sight without the sense of touch to help it; the sense of touch without the sense of sight; in fact hearing, alone, without the aid of any other sense whatever, or with the aid of a diseased portion of one entire sense, could not have proved so stupid. Where is the guilty flush that should suffuse your face? If, even in the bosom of an elderly woman, such fiendish desires lie dormant, ready to break out at any moment into uncontrollable rebellion, how volatile must be the chastity of a young man; no wonder it dissipates in the ardent fire that consumes him. Henceforth count it no disgrace when youth is carried away by the fierce strength of its passions, for here we see that in age, when passion is supposed to be as cold as ice, it may glow just as fiercely, and that mature judgment, instead of restraining, may minister to the impulses.

**Queen:** O, my son, spare me the rest. You force me to search the very depths of my heart, and to discover there foul and permanent blemishes that never can be removed. Spare me the rest. Every syllable you utter pierces my ear like a sword thrust. Be silent now, my dear Hamlet.

**Hamlet:** An assassin, a deliberate scoundrel, a serf, one who is nothing in comparison to your former husband, a mere buffoon king, who had not sufficient courage to seize the kingdom and its sway by violence, but, like a petty thief, stealthily filched the costly crown and hid it away!

**Queen:** O spare me, I pray!

**Hamlet:** A clown aping the character of a monarch!

*[Enter ghost.]*

Angels above! draw near and shield me from all harm! What is your purpose in coming thus, O benevolent form?

**Queen:** Ah, me! he has taken leave of his senses altogether.

**Hamlet:** Have you made this visit in order to rebuke me for indulging in mere outbursts of feeling, and allowing the opportunity to glide by for carrying out the momentous duty so solemnly imposed upon me? Tell me.

**Ghost:** Remember my words. I have come to reanimate the strength of your resolution, now nearly forgotten. But see, the utmost perplexity has taken possession of your mother. Go to her aid and save her from the doubts which devour her. Imagination exerts most sway over those who are physically weakest. Say something to her, Hamlet.

**Hamlet:** What is the matter with you, mother?

**Queen:** Ah, my son, say rather what is the matter with you, that you stare so steadfastly at nothing, and carry on a conversation with empty space. Your entire soul seems to shine out in astonishment at your eyes. Your matted locks, erstwhile so flat, stand upright on your head like slumbering warriors awakened by some signal of danger; excrescences endowed with life. O, my good Hamlet, endeavor to moderate the burning vehemence of your disorder by the exercise of calm restraint. Tell me what you gaze upon.

**Hamlet:** Do you not see him? Behold his wan expression as he gazes with piercing eyes upon us. His appearance, combined with the reason for it, would not appeal in vain even to things inanimate, but would make them susceptible. Gaze not upon me thus, else you will move me to such compassion that I shall be unable to carry out my austere intentions. Then the task imposed upon me will lose its proper character, and I shall shed tears only, instead of shedding blood.

**Queen:** Who is it you address?

**Hamlet:** What do you see as you look before you?

**Queen:** I see everything that is there, and yet not what you see.

**Hamlet:** What words assail your ears?

**Queen:** None but the words we speak to each other.

**Hamlet:** See there then, my father! Notice how gradually he vanishes from sight. He is in his dress as when alive. See him now, he is just passing through the doorway!

*[Exit ghost.]*

**Queen:** This is nothing but a creature of your imagination. Insanity is exceedingly skilful in inventing such illusory images.

**Hamlet:** I am not in the least degree insane. My heart beats at its normal healthy rate, no quicker than your own. The words I have just said are not those of a madman. Try me in any way you think proper. I can repeat them over word for word, whereas an idiot would wander playfully from the subject. Mother, as you hope for God's mercy, do not deceive yourself with the comforting assurance that it was my insanity and not your sin that caused my furious outburst. To do so will be merely to place a surface covering over your fault, not to cure it, whilst rapid putrefaction, gnawing your soul to its very center, secretly poisons it. Openly acknowledge to your Maker that you have erred, express contrition for your past misdeeds, and determine to shun such conduct in the future, and whatever you do, do not add to the enormity of your offences by further indulgence. Pray excuse the candor of my righteous reproof, for in this gross and pampered age even righteousness must ask forgiveness of wickedness, yes, and bow and beg, too, for permission to do him a service.

**Queen:** Hamlet, my son, my heart is torn asunder by thy reproof.

**Hamlet:** Then cast aside the viler portion of it, and lead a life so much the holier for its loss. Farewell, mother. Do not, however, go to your husband's room tonight. Behave as though you had become a changed woman, even if as yet the feeling is somewhat lacking. That demon usage, the evil genius of our habits, who destroys all the finer feelings, confers, however, this benefit upon us, that he gives to the repeated performance of good actions an ease and readiness in so doing that is rapidly acquired. Stay away this time, and you will find it less difficult to stay away again, and still less difficult to stay away the third time. For custom is nearly capable of producing a complete change in a man's character, and with its aid the evil one may either be overpowered or cast out with resistless force. Farewell a second time, and when you feel moved to ask God's pardon and forgiveness, I will come and crave your blessing.

As to Polonius here [*pointing to Polonius*], I am deeply sorry for my rashness, but it seems as if I had been ordained by God to be the instrument of his death, so that I might suffer through him, and he through me. I will see that the body is disposed of, and will fully justify my action in killing him. Once more, farewell. Though my conduct to you may seem harsh, it is solely for your benefit that it is so. And my harsh conduct to you is nothing to what I may expect to receive at the hands of the king. Let me make one final request before I go, dear mother.

**Queen:** What is it?

**Hamlet:** That you will on no account do what I forbade you to do, that is, allow your coarse husband to entice you to his room, smother you with playful caresses, address you by endearing names, so that in return for a couple of his foul kisses, or the touch of his hateful fingers about your neck, you permit him to extort my secret from you that I am, as a matter of fact, not in the least degree insane, but that I have cunningly feigned to be so.

Of course you ought to tell him. You are only a woman of the most exalted rank, endowed with beauty, gravity, and wisdom, so how could you possibly keep important matters like these from the knowledge of such a toad, a bat, a tomcat as is your husband? Throwing discretion and concealment to the winds you would imitate the monkey of the story who removed a basket of live birds from the roof of a house, allowed the birds to escape, and getting in himself, proceeded to try an experiment whether he could fly like them, and jumped out and killed himself.

**Queen:** You may depend upon my saying nothing about it. If my secret could escape from me merely by breathing, I would die for want of breath rather than make it known even in that way.

**Hamlet:** I am to be sent off to England; I suppose you know that?

**Queen:** Alas, yes. You remind me that such is his majesty's determination.

**Hamlet:** The messages that are to accompany me are already signed, and my escort is to consist of the two companions of my youth. These men, to whose care I can commit my life with as much confidence as I could commit it to poisonous snakes, have been chosen by the king so that I may be the more easily led to a villainous end. Well, let them go on with their plot. It is a splendid joke to see the engineer blown up into the air with his own instrument of destruction, and it will be a remarkable thing if I do not contrive a deeper plot than theirs, which will bring them to utter ruin. It is a glorious sight to see two deep-laid plots come into direct opposition with each other. This body here forces me to contrive what is best to be done with it. I'll haul it into a room close by. Farewell, mother. This minister of state has now more calmness, reservation and gravity than ever he had in his lifetime, for he certainly was a silly prattling rogue. This way, my lord, let me bring this business to a close. Farewell, my lady.

[*Exit separately, Hamlet dragging Polonius.*]

# ACT IV · SCENE 1

*[A room in the castle.]*

*[Enter king, queen, Rosencrantz and Guildenstern.]*

**King:** You plainly indicate by your audible respiration, and the agitation which disturbs your nature to its very depths, that you know something. Tell it to us, then, for it is right and proper that we should know it. What have you done with Hamlet?

**Queen:** Be good enough to let us have the room to ourselves for a few moments.

*[Exit Rosencrantz and Guildenstern.]*

O, my dear husband, I have had a most dreadful experience this night.

**King:** Why, my queen, what is the matter with your son?

**Queen:** He is as wild as the ocean and the gale when these two elements struggle for the mastery. In this burst of insanity, he heard a rustling sound proceeding from behind the hangings, and hastily drawing his sword, and exclaiming "a spy, a spy," in a fit of imaginary fear, he slew the innocent Polonius, who lay concealed there.

**King:** Alas, this is an offence of the utmost gravity. I would have fared no better myself had I been in Polonius' place. As long as he is allowed to roam about unrestrained, neither you nor I, nor, in fact, anyone can consider himself safe. Ah, me, in what way shall we account for this horrid murder? We shall be blamed for lack of foresight in not having curtailed the liberty of this crazy young prince, and kept him from coming into the company of others. In our affectionate regard for him, we deliberately refused to take proper precautions, acting like someone afflicted with a loathsome complaint, who, rather than let it be known, allows the disease to eat away the most vital parts of his body. In what direction shall we look for him?

**Queen:** I left him dragging away the corpse of the murdered man, and shedding tears of sorrow for his act, showing that even his insanity has a touch of soundness in it, which here exhibits itself like a vein of precious metal in a mine of baser ones.

**King:** O, my queen, let us withdraw. As soon as day begins to break, he must sail away from here, while we, striving our very utmost, and using all the authority which we owe to

75

our position, will endeavor to gloss over and extenuate this dreadful crime. Here, Guildenstern!

*[Re-enter Rosencrantz and Guildenstern.]*

My two friends, kindly obtain the assistance of some others. Our son has taken Polonius' life in one of his insane outbursts, and has removed the body from the queen's chamber to some place of concealment. Find out where he is. Use no violent language to him, but see that the corpse is conveyed to the sanctuary. Do this as quickly as possible now, I beseech you.

*[Exit Rosencrantz and Guildenstern.]*

Now, my wife, let us call together our most discreet counsellors, and acquaint them with our intentions with regard to this inopportune event. If we do this, the base insinuations of slander, which travel from one end of the world to another as quickly and unerringly as a gunshot flies to its target, may avoid us altogether, and strike only the air, which cannot feel the blow. Let us go. This mishap has filled my mind with hesitation and misgiving.

*[Exit.]*

## ACT IV · SCENE 2

*[Another room in the castle.]*
*[Enter Hamlet.]*

**Hamlet:** Well disposed of, at last.

**Rosencrantz:**
**Guildenstern:** } *[Within.]* Prince Hamlet! My lord!

**Hamlet:** Stay a moment, what can that sound be? Someone is calling me by name. Ah! They are coming this way.

*[Enter Rosencrantz and Guildenstern.]*

**Rosencrantz:** Where have you put the corpse, your lordship?

**Hamlet:** I have mixed it with the earth to which, by nature, it is related.

**Rosencrantz:** Do let us know where you have put it, for we wish to take it away from here and place it in the church.

**Hamlet:** Wherever did you get that notion from?

**Rosencrantz:** What notion?

**Hamlet:** That I will divulge my own secrets but keep yours. Again, fancy being questioned by one who wishes to get as much information from me as possible in order to give it to someone else. What reply ought a royal prince to make to a fellow like that?

**Rosencrantz:** Is that your opinion of me, your lordship?

**Hamlet:** Yes, it is. You will do anything to secure the royal favor, together with the rewards and attributes of power that such favor brings. After all, such servants as yourselves are really the most useful his majesty possesses. He keeps you always at hand as a monkey does with the nuts he takes into his mouth first, intending to eat last. Whenever the king requires the information you have picked up for him, he merely compresses you as he would a sponge, and you are ready to be used again.

**Rosencrantz:** I am quite at a loss to know your meaning, your lordship.

**Hamlet:** I am rejoiced to hear it. Fools never can understand the intention of a roguish remark.

**Rosencrantz:** We were commanded, your lordship, to enquire what you have done with the corpse, and also to bring you to his majesty's presence.

**Hamlet:** The corpse now keeps company with its true and lawful sovereign, but he who calls himself monarch is not near it. Who is this king?

**Guildenstern:** Who is he, your lordship?

**Hamlet:** A mere cipher. Lead me to his presence. It's hidden now. Let us all seek it.

*[Exit.]*

# ACT IV · SCENE 3

*[Another room in the castle.]*
*[Enter king and his attendants.]*

**King:** They are looking for him now to find out what he has done with the corpse. As long as he is allowed to retain his liberty, no one can consider himself safe. But what am I to do? The foolish common people, who are guided in their likes and dislikes by mere outward appearances and not by reason, are so passionately devoted to him that it would be very unwise on our part to employ the full force of the law against him. For in a case like this they only consider the severe punishment their idol is suffering, and not the crime that has led to it. In order then to avoid this source of friction, his banishment from our shores must appear to be the outcome of calm deliberation. When a malady has reached such an acute stage as his, the patient can be eased only by the application of a very drastic remedy.

*[Enter Rosencrantz.]*

Well, what has happened now?

**Rosencrantz:** We have utterly failed, my lord, in our attempts to find out what he has done with the corpse.

**King:** Have you brought him here?

**Rosencrantz:** Yes, he is outside, under an escort, awaiting your highness' commands.

**King:** Usher him into our presence.

**Rosencrantz:** Here, Guildenstern, come forward with Prince Hamlet.

*[Enter Hamlet and Guildenstern.]*

**King:** Hamlet, you must let us know where Polonius is.

**Hamlet:** He is in attendance at a banquet.

**King:** What banquet?

**Hamlet:** A banquet at which he is not a partaker but is partaken of. A congress of discriminating worms is, at this very moment, engaged upon him. Our friend the worm is the only real monarch of all that pertains to food. We feed all living things well in order to provide good nourishment for ourselves, and we nourish our own bodies merely to provide food for worms. To these creatures a stout monarch and an emaciated vagrant form merely two different courses of the same meal. That is what it amounts to.

**King:** How sad it is to hear him ramble thus!

**Hamlet:** It is quite possible for an angler to bait his hook with a worm that has partaken of some dead sovereign. Yes, and afterward, make a meal of the fish that swallowed the worm.

**King:** Well, to what end do you mention this fact?

**Hamlet:** Merely to demonstrate how it is quite possible for a monarch to make a journey of state through the intestines of a beggar.

**King:** Tell us where Polonius is.

**Hamlet:** Send someone to the realms above to see if he is there, and if they fail to discover him, go down below and look for him yourself. However, if you search for him for more than two or three weeks without result, he will become distinctly perceptible to your sense of smell whenever you ascend the stairs that lead to the hall.

**King:** See if you can find him there.

*[To some attendants.]*

**Hamlet:** You need not be afraid of his running away.

*[Exit attendants.]*

**King:** Hamlet, this rash act of yours makes it imperative for your own personal welfare, which is ever the object of our regard, however much we may deplore your action, that you should leave this land with the utmost haste. Make, then, the needful preparations; the ship awaits you, the breeze is favorable, your companions in travel are ready to accompany you, and, in fact, there is nothing to hinder you from setting sail for England at once.

**Hamlet:** England, did you say?

**King:** Yes, England.

**Hamlet:** Very well.

**King:** If you knew all, you would indeed say so.

**Hamlet:** I am at this moment gazing upon a loving angel who knows all. Enough of this. England is now my goal. Good-bye, beloved mother.

**King:** You mean "father," my son.

**Hamlet:** Not at all. Have you not married my mother, and those who are married, do they not become one? Therefore you must be my mother. Enough. I am off to England.

*[Exit.]*

**King:** Stick close to his heels and induce him to embark immediately. He must leave the coast of Denmark before daybreak. After him now, for all other matters connected with this business are signed and settled. Be as quick as you can, I beseech you.

*[Exit Rosencrantz and Guildenstern.]*

With regard to thee, O England, if thou carest at all for my friendship—and the strength of my might may well teach thee to do so, for the wounds thou hast received at the hands of our nation are still so fresh in thy remembrance that thou continuest to show a respect for us which is no longer enforced by arms—thou hadst better not regard with indifference this our royal command, the purport of which is fully explained in the letters which accompany and agree with it, to wit, that Hamlet must be instantly executed. Comply with it, England, for his existence has the same effect upon me as a continual fever has upon the blood, and I look to thee for relief. Till I am assured that my orders have been carried out, I shall be unable to consider myself happy, whatever chance may befall me.

*[Exit.]*

## ACT IV · SCENE 4

*[A plain in Denmark.]*
*[Enter Fortinbras, a captain and soldiers, marching.]*

**Fortinbras:** Officer, bear my respects to the ruler of this realm and inform him that, subject to his majesty's permission, and in accordance with the terms of his agreement, Fortinbras begs to be allowed to transport his troops across his dominions. Meet me at the appointed place. Should the king of Denmark desire to say something to us we will attend personally and swear loyalty to him. Give him to understand this.

**Captain:** It shall be done, your highness.

**Fortinbras:** Proceed slowly forward.

*[Exit Fortinbras and soldiers.]*
*[Enter Hamlet, Rosencrantz, Guildenstern and others.]*

**Hamlet:** To whom do these troops belong, my friend?

**Captain:** To the Norwegian king, sir.

**Hamlet:** Tell me, I beg, where they are bound.

**Captain:** They go to fight the Poles.

**Hamlet:** Who is the leader of the expedition?

**Captain:** Fortinbras, the nephew of the reigning prince.

**Hamlet:** Is the enterprise against the country as a whole, or merely against some part of its borders?

**Captain:** Well, sir, to tell the truth without the least exaggeration, the plot of land we go to conquer is so small, that the only value it has lies in the honor of saying that it is ours. The least of it is not worth the rent of five ducats, only five. Indeed, if it were sold outright, it would profit neither of the combatants to any great extent.

**Hamlet:** Surely the Poles will consider the plot not worth fighting about.

**Captain:** On the contrary, it is well defended even at this moment.

**Hamlet:** Then, you mean to tell me, that to decide who shall possess this worthless piece of territory will require a sacrifice of more than two thousand human lives, and an expenditure of ten times that number of ducats. Truly, this eagerness to quarrel about nothing is the outcome of prosperity, and immunity from war too long continued. And like an abscess which bursts internally and results in death without showing any outward symptoms of disease, it shows that all is not well with the state. I am heartily obliged to you for your explanation.

**Captain:** Heaven preserve you, my lord!

*[Exit.]*

**Rosencrantz:** Will you oblige us by proceeding, your lordship?

**Hamlet:** I shall overtake you without loss of time if you go forward a few steps.

*[Exit all but Hamlet.]*

Is it not remarkable how every little incident that occurs seems publicly to accuse my irresolution in pursuing my vengeance? Do we not debase our nature to a level as low as that of the brute creation when we employ our time in no other business than that of slumbering and eating? The Creator, who endowed us with such wide and comprehensive faculties, capable of recalling the past and anticipating the future, never surely intended that these gifts, which we possess in common with Himself, should be allowed to grow mouldy from want of use. What is it, then, which makes me unwilling to perform an action that is my plain duty? It may be mere brutelike forgetfulness, or some cowardly feeling of reluctance caused by pondering too minutely over the consequences of my action, in meditations which contain very little of common sense and a great deal of cowardice. I cannot understand it. The motive, the desire, the ability and the opportunity for action are all present with me.

Not only so, but similar instances, so obvious that the most stupid intellect could not fail to see their resemblance to my own, urge me on. Take this expedition, for instance, so powerful and costly, commanded by a youth of royal blood, unaccustomed to a life of deprivation and hardship, and yet inspired by a god like unrest. His enthusiasm, scorning all possible consequences, openly ventures all that is liable to loss and destruction to whatever fate mortality or risk may chance to bring—and all for the merest trifle. 'Tis not the mark of true nobility to take offence on every trifling occasion of dispute, but when our personal character is assailed, it is the mark of true nobility to take offence then upon the slightest provocation.

What am I to think of myself, then? My father has been murdered and my mother's fair name sullied, two causes which are in themselves sufficient to stir both my judgment and my passion, and yet I take no action, though, to my everlasting reproach, twenty thousand men before my very eyes go as calmly to almost sure destruction as they would go to bed, for nothing more than a mere fanciful point of honor, a piece of land not large enough to afford standing room for the men who are to fight for it, or even to be a burial ground for those who will perish in the fray. After this, let me swear to entertain none but murderous intentions—all others are useless.

[*Exit.*]

## ACT IV · SCENE 5
[*Elsinore. A room in the castle.*]
[*Enter queen, Horatio and a gentleman.*]

**Queen:** I refuse to have anything to say to her.

**Gentleman:** She is most urgent in her requests. I may add, quite crazy. One cannot help feeling sympathy for her condition.

**Queen:** What is it she desires?

**Gentleman:** She babbles continuously about her deceased parent; declares that strange things are happening in the world about her, and presses and smites her bosom. She kicks spitefully at the smallest obstruction in her path; what she says is couched in such ambiguous language that half of it cannot possibly be understood. Her language is a mere succession of meaningless words; yet, haphazard as they are, one cannot refrain from trying to put them together so as to make sense. Those who listen to her find themselves compelled to guess at their meaning, and then to make an unskilful attempt to suit the words to it. And as far as one can thus gather from them, and from the motions of the eyelids and head with which they are accompanied, one is forced to the conclusion that some great misfortune has happened to her of which she possesses but a dim consciousness.

**Horatio:** I think you had better speak to her, for her words may suggest thoughts to those who are fond of hatching mischief, which may be filled with harmful consequences to your majesties.

**Queen:** Well, then, admit her.

*[Exit gentleman.]*

[*Aside.*] In my present state, as is always the case with a guilty person, each trifling event seems to be but the forerunner of some terrible disaster. The wicked are so tormented with needless suspicion that they betray themselves, in seeking to avoid betrayal.

*[Re-enter gentleman, with Ophelia.]*

**Ophelia:** Bring me into the presence of Denmark's fair queen.

**Queen:** Well, Ophelia, what do you wish? Tell me.

**Ophelia:** [*Sings.*] In what way may I recognize the man who is really devoted to you amongst a host of others? He will be dressed like a pilgrim, with shells in his headgear, sandals on his feet, and a staff in his hand.

**Queen:** Ah, me! Dear Ophelia, what is the meaning of your song?

**Ophelia:** What do you say? You do not understand. Let me request you to attend, then. [*Sings.*] He lives no longer, but has departed, leaving this world behind, your majesty. His humble grass-grown grave bears at its foot a tablet to his memory. Alas!

**Queen:** Stay, Ophelia, hear me—

**Ophelia:** Listen again, I beg. [*Sings.*] Enveloped in a winding sheet as pure in color as the snow on the hilltops—

*[Enter king.]*

**Queen:** Behold this piteous sight, your majesty.

**Ophelia:** [*Sings.*] And thickly covered with beautiful flowers he was borne to his tomb, his faithful lover shedding the while abundant tears of grief.

**King:** What ails you, my sweet child?

**Ophelia:** Heaven reward you, sir! People relate how the child of the baker was transformed into an owl. We are acquainted with our present condition, but what will become of us is known only to Thee, O God. May He be present when you partake of food!

**King:** Her parent's death occupies her thoughts.

**Ophelia:** Do not let us quarrel about the matter, I beg. Should you be requested to explain it, merely reply as follows: [*Sings.*] The festival of St. Valentine will be celebrated in the morning, and at break of day you will find me awaiting your appearance, so that I may become your true love.

**King:** Has she suffered in this way for any considerable time?

**Ophelia:** I trust that everything has happened for the best. We must bear it as well as we can. Yet I am unable to withhold my tears at the thought of his resting place in the cheerless earth. I will acquaint Laertes with what has occurred, and before I go, let me say how grateful I am for your advising me so well. Now, call my carriage! Farewell, good dames! Fairwell, fair dames. Farewell, farewell.

[*Exit.*]

**King:** Do not lose sight of her for an instant, and I beseech you observe her carefully. [*Exit Horatio.*] What a terrible change profound sorrow has wrought in her! It is entirely caused by the loss of her parent.

O, my dear Gertrude, misfortunes never make their appearance one at a time, like scouts, but whole armies seem to arrive at once. Take our case, for instance. To begin with, Polonius meets with his death, then Hamlet, whose headstrong action was the cause of it, is banished, as he richly deserved to be. Moreover, Polonius' death stirs up much bad blood among the people, who express their disapproval in low murmurings of evil, and we make matters worse by burying him in secrecy and in haste. Again, his unfortunate child, by taking leave of her senses, has parted with her most precious possession, lacking which we have only the outward semblance of humanity, or are reduced to the level of the brute creation.

Finally, and as important as all the foregoing put together, Laertes, who has returned to Denmark without announcing the fact to us, ponders over the amazement caused by his father's death, and is reserved and mysterious in his conduct, while numerous whisperers poison his thoughts with mischievous stories as to the manner in which Polonius met his doom; stories in which the accusers, being obliged to substantiate their statements in some way, do not hesitate even to accuse me to everyone they meet. O, Gertrude, Gertrude, these calamities come upon me like a discharge of cannon-shot. Each one by itself is capable of bringing me to utter ruin.

*[A noise within.]*

**Queen:** Woe is me! Whatever does this tumult mean?

**King:** Summon my bodyguard and bid them guard the entrance.

*[Enter another gentleman.]*

What has happened?

**Gentleman:** Take measures to ensure your safety, your majesty. The sea, when it rises above its proper boundary, does not cover the level stretches of country with more furious speed than that with which the youthful Laertes, followed by a rebellious throng in arms, overpowers your commanders. The mob already acknowledge his authority, and just as if we were at the very commencement of this earth's career, and there were no such things as times past or ancient usage, things which should support and sanction every new watchword, they exclaim, "We have decided; Laertes shall reign over us." They receive their own decision with great acclamation, throwing up their hats, clapping their hands and shouting with all their might, "Laertes shall reign over us, Laertes shall reign!"

**Queen:** With what alacrity these hounds give tongue upon the wrong scent! You are following the trail in the wrong direction, you unfaithful sons of Denmark.

**King:** They have forced an entrance.

*[Noise within.]*
*[Enter Laertes, armed; Danes following.]*

**Laertes:** Is this despicable monarch in here? Gentlemen, remain outside awhile.

**Danes:** Nay, we will enter with you.

**Laertes:** Let me enter alone, I beg.

**Danes:** As you please, sir.

*[They retire to outside the door.]*

**Laertes:** I am obliged to you. Watch all possible entrances by which help may come to the king. Most wicked monarch, what hast thou done with my father?

**Queen:** Control yourself, my dear Laertes.

**King:** How is it, Laertes, that I find you at the head of a revolt of such magnitude? Do not try to restrain him, Gertrude. No harm can possibly come to me. A monarch is so encircled by divine protection that traitors are unable to approach him to carry out their wicked intentions, but can merely look, as it were, over the fence that intervenes between themselves and the object of their designs. Now, Laertes, what makes you so angry? Do not attempt to hold him back, Gertrude. Say what you have to say, sir.

**Laertes:** What have you done with my father?

**King:** He has met with his death.

**Queen:** But my husband was not the author of it.

**King:** Do not prevent him from fully stating his claim.

**Laertes:** What caused his death? Come, it is no use trying to cajole me. Utterly forsaking all duty I owe to my sovereign, turning my back completely upon every oath of loyalty I have sworn, regardless alike of religious feeling and the prompting of my own inward mentor, I am willing, in this cause, to jeopardize the safety of my very soul. Here I make my unalterable decision, that whatever be the result of my action in this world, or the world to come, I will exact a most complete and satisfying vengeance for my father's death.

**King:** Will anything restrain you?

**Laertes:** Nothing in the whole earth but my own determination. The resources that I have at my disposal for so doing may not be great, but I will make the best of them, and be so careful, that, though small, they will go a long way.

**King:** And, my kind friend, supposing you get to know the true facts about the murder of your beloved parent, have you made up your mind that, like the winner of a sweepstake, who gathers up all the deposits, you will include everyone in your vengeance, innocent as well as guilty?

**Laertes:** I will include none save the guilty.

**King:** Would you care to learn who they are?

**Laertes:** Those who have been really true to him will I cherish with deepest affection, and, like the pelican that draws blood from her own breast to nourish her young ones, I shall, as it were, feed them with my love.

**King:** Well, you are at last uttering sentiments compatible alike with filial duty and perfect courtesy. I am able to make it as clear to your mental perception as daylight is to your physical, that I am not only innocent of any connection with the decease of your parent, but that I am more deeply grieved by it than anyone, saving yourself.

**Danes:** [*Within.*] Permit her to enter.

**Laertes:** Now then! What is this disturbance?

[*Re-enter Ophelia.*]

May the burning fire in my head consume the seat of my intellect, and may tears, many times as bitter as those which now fall from me, completely destroy my power of sight! As I live I shall obtain such redress for the deed which caused thy insanity that the balance shall be in our favor. O, loved one, in the first blush of youth. Ah, Ophelia, my tender and affectionate sister! Would anyone have ever thought that the understanding of this young girl was just as liable to destruction as the life of her aged father? Where affection is concerned the disposition is so delicately tender that some valuable function, as an example of itself, is sure to follow the object of its regard.

**Ophelia:** [*Sings.*] They carried him to his rest with uncovered face, hey, nonny, nonny, and wept copiously with sorrow for their lost one. Good-bye to you, my loved one.

**Laertes:** If thou wast in full possession of thy senses, and did eloquently entreat me to pursue my vengeance, thy words could not carry so much weight as this rambling speech of thine.

**Ophelia:** [*Sings.*] If you name him a-down-a, you ought to sing a-down-a-down.

This song sounds best when sung accompanied by the spinning wheel. It is about the unjust bailiff who eloped with the daughter of his employer.

**Laertes:** These meaningless words of hers are more touching than any sensible ones could be.

**Ophelia:** Here is some rosemary for you. It is a symbol of memory. Please cherish his memory, brother dear; and here are pansies also; they signify thoughts.

**Laertes:** She instructs us, mad though she is. Memory and thoughts are rightly allotted.

**Ophelia:** I have some fennel to give you, and some columbines also; and see, take this rue as well, and I will keep some of it for myself. You must give your rue its Sunday name, which signifies God's mercy and forgiveness, to distinguish it from mine, which can never be anything to me but mere sorrow. Here is a daisy for you. I would have offered you some violets if they had not all faded at my father's death.

They told me he died at peace with all men.

    [*Sings.*] For my only delight is in my dear handsome Robin.

**Laertes:** Anxiety, distress, suffering and thoughts even more terrible than these, are rendered attractive and beautiful by the language in which she clothes them.

**Ophelia:** [*Sings.*] Will he never return? Return no more to thee? Ah, no! His life is sped, and however long thou may live, he will return to thee no more. His hair was of the purest whiteness, and his head the color of flax. Gone forever is he now; tears and sighs are useless. May the Lord grant him rest and peace! And all the faithful departed too! This is my prayer. Good-bye to you all.

                                                     [*Exit.*]

**Laertes:** In the name of heaven, is not this a heart-rending sight?

**King:** If you decline, Laertes, to allow me to share your sorrows, you do me a great injustice. Just withdraw for a few moments and choose whom you please amongst the most discreet of those who are attached to you. Let them weigh the evidence and decide the matter at issue between us. If their verdict is that I am in any way implicated in the guilt of Polonius' death, I am willing to forfeit my realm, my sovereignty, my existence and, in fact, everything I possess in order to recompense you. If, on the other hand, I am proved to be innocent, give your calm attention to what I have to say, and you will find that I am anxious to help you in every way to obtain the full satisfaction for which your spirit longs.

**Laertes:** I am willing to do as you suggest. But he died in so strange a manner; his burial was so secret; his grave is so entirely devoid of a memorial of any kind, not even his weapons or his armorial bearings being hung on it; his funeral was attended by none of the pomp which his rank might justly claim; all these seem to me like the voice of my father calling to me from heaven and they compel me to inquire into their meaning.

**King:** And enquiries shall be made. Then let the full weight of your vengeance fall upon the real culprit. Let me beseech you to follow me.

                                                   [*Exit.*]

## ACT IV · SCENE 6

*[Another room in the castle.]*
*[Enter Horatio and a servant.]*

**Horatio:** Who are the men that desire to see me?

**Servant:** They are sailors, sir; and they tell me they have written communications to give you.

**Horatio:** Send them this way.

*[Exit servant.]*

I am sure I know no one who could send a letter to me from abroad, except Prince Hamlet.

*[Enter sailors.]*

**First Sailor:** May the Lord prosper you, sir!

**Horatio:** I heartily reciprocate that wish.

**First Sailor:** It shall be granted, sir, if it be His pleasure to do so. I have a communication to give you, sir. It was entrusted to me by the envoy who recently set sail for England, and I was told to give it to one Horatio, whom I am given to understand I am addressing.

**Horatio:** [*Reads.*] "Horatio, after you have read this letter, see that the bearers are ushered into his majesty's presence, for they have some dispatches for him too. Our voyage had scarcely lasted two days, when were were pursued by a piratical vessel that was fitted out in a thoroughly offensive fashion. As we discovered that she outsailed us easily, there was nothing for it but to pluck up our courage and prepare to meet her. As soon as we had thrown out our grapnels, I jumped on board, but just as I did so, the two ships parted and I became their only captive. They treated me very well for pirates, but had good reasons for doing so, for I have promised in return to do them a service.

See that his majesty receives the letters that they bear, and then make your way to me as quickly as though you were trying to escape from death. I have something to tell you privately which will render you speechless with amazement, and yet no words of mine would be sufficient to describe what I have to tell. The bearers of my message will conduct you to my whereabouts. I left my two old schoolfellows to continue their voyage. I have a great deal to tell you about them also. Good-bye. He, of whose attachment to thee thou art well aware, *Hamlet*."

Follow me and I will provide you with an opportunity of

delivering your dispatches, and I shall make the more haste over it, in order that you may lead me to him who sent thee.

[*Exit.*]

## ACT IV · SCENE 7

[*Another room in the castle.*]
[*Enter king and Laertes.*]

**King:** Surely now you can hardly refrain from endorsing my innocence, which has been so completely proved. Not only so, but you will count me as one of your allies, for your intelligent comprehension cannot fail to have grasped the fact that the murderer of your illustrious parent sought to kill me also.

**Laertes:** Yes, that is quite plain to me now. Still, I cannot understand your reason for not taking measures to punish offences so criminal in your character, and so justly deserving of death. One would have thought that regard for your own security, the promptings of your own judgment and everything in fact besides, would have urged you to pursue such a course.

**King:** Well, my motives for so doing were mainly twofold. They will probably appear to you to be two weak ones, but I assure you they carry great weight with me.

First then, my wife is so devoted to her son that she cannot bear even to lose sight of him, and I do not know whether it is something worthy of praise or merely troublesome, but for my part, I am bound to confess that she is so much a part of my very existence that just as a star can have no motion save that of the crystal globe to which it is attached, so I have none except in conjunction with her. My second reason for not openly prosecuting him is the great estimation in which he is held by the common people. These, after the fashion of the well which petrifies wooden articles deposited in its waters, glaze all his shortcomings over with their love for him, and would see in the very fetters with which he was bound a further reason for lavishing their affection upon him. In this way, then, my plan for his punishment not being strong enough to endure the opposition which it would encounter, would simply become a means of making myself unpopular, instead of the person against whom it was directed.

**Laertes:** And the consequence of this, is that my honored parent has been taken from me and my sister deprived of her reason, a sister, if I may extol her former state rather than her present one, whose excellences were so numerous that they seemed to defy all modern times to produce a being so faultless as she. Still, I am determined to avenge them.

**King:** Do not allow your fears, lest you be disappointed, to cause you a moment's uneasiness. Our nature is not so entirely spiritless and inactive that we can allow something to menace us in front of our eyes and treat it as a mere joke. You have yet to learn the measures I have taken. I had a personal affection for your father, and I have also some regard for myself. You will be able to gather from these two facts—

[*Enter a messenger.*]

What brings you here? Tell me your message.

**Messenger:** These communications, your majesty, are from Prince Hamlet. This is for yourself, and this is for his mother.

**King:** There is surely some mistake. By whom were they conveyed hither?

**Messenger:** I did not see the bearers myself, but those who did, tell me they were seafaring men. Claudio handed them to me, and they were given to him by the person who conveyed them hither.

**King:** I shall let you know their contents, Laertes. You may go.

[*Exit messenger.*]

[*Reads.*] "To the most exalted and powerful majesty of Denmark. This communication will inform you that I have landed without resources upon your shores. I intend tomorrow to request an interview with your highness, and at this interview I shall, after having obtained your gracious permission to do so, give a full account of the circumstances which have led to my coming back in a manner so unexpected and still more surprising.— *Hamlet.*" Whatever, I wonder, is the signification of this? Have his companions returned with him, too? Stay, perhaps it is all some strange delusion, and he has not returned at all.

**Laertes:** Is the handwriting familiar to you?

**King:** O yes, the handwriting is his. Without money! And look, he adds a note at the end saying he is by himself. What advice have you to offer?

**Laertes:** It thoroughly perplexes me, your majesty. But what of his arrival? My drooping spirits are kindling already at the thought that, after all, I shall be able to charge him before his very face with his crimes.

**King:** If he has really returned, which seems hardly possible in face of the measures I took, and yet just as impossible to think otherwise with this letter in my hand; are you willing to be entirely guided by my advice?

**Laertes:** I am quite willing, your majesty, provided only that your advice does not involve my reconciliation with him.

**King:** It involves only a reconciliation with yourself. If it is really true that he has come back because he shrinks from such a journey, and if nothing will induce him to return, I will undertake to persuade him to take part in a scheme which I have just brought to perfection in my thoughts, in the course of which he cannot fail to meet with his death, and yet no suspicion of foul play will ever light upon us. Even the queen, who loves him so well, will not be able to accuse us of treachery, but will say it was unavoidable.

**Laertes:** I shall be more willing to be guided by your advice if you can possibly manage to make me the instrument by which it is carried out.

**King:** It so happens that I can. During your stay in France, one of the accomplishments in which you particularly excel has been the subject of much conversation, and that, too, when Hamlet was present. All your other accomplishments combined did not excite his emulation to so great an extent as this one, though in my estimation it is the one least worthy to be proud of.

**Laertes:** Tell me what it was, your lordship.

**King:** One of the paltry adornments of young men, but a necessary one, I suppose, since the dashing and showy dress of a young man is just as suitable to his age as are the fur-trimmed robes of an elderly man, which betoken gravity and prosperity.

Some weeks ago, we were visited by a young Norman. I have met many Frenchmen, and, indeed, have fought against them, so I know what skilful equestrians they are. This courtier's horsemanship, however, was nothing short of marvellous. He seemed to be riveted to his saddle, and performed such remarkable feats there that, centaurlike, he and his gallant steed seemed to be one and the same creature. Indeed, he was so much superior to everything I had ever imagined, that any fanciful feats of dexterity that I could have invented would have been inferior to those which he actually performed.

**Laertes:** He was from Normandy, you say?

**King:** He was.

**Laertes:** Why, it must have been Lamond.

**King:** Yes, that was the name.

**Laertes:** I am intimately acquainted with him. He is a most brilliant gentleman, in fact, the fairest ornament of France.

**King:** He admitted, however, your science and skill in all games dealing with the protection of the person, and most especially in the management of the foil. Indeed, he was so impressed with your consummate skill in the use of that weapon, that he declared a bout between yourself and a worthy opponent would be worth going some distance to see. The fencers of France, he confidently affirmed, seemed, when in competition with yourself, to lose all powers of attack and defence, and all the quickness of sight so necessary in this exercise. Well, Laertes, this account of your skill roused in the mind of Hamlet such a feeling of jealousy that there was nothing he longed or prayed for so much as your unexpected arrival in Denmark, in order that he might arrange a match with you.

**Laertes:** What plan can you suggest, your lordship?

**King:** Laertes, is your love for your father really deep-seated and genuine? Or do you rather resemble the picture of a person in grief, a mere sorrowful countenance, without any real feeling behind it?

**Laertes:** Tell me the reason for your question.

**King:** It is not because I doubt the affection you bore him, but because it is a fact that all affection has a beginning, and abundant instances occur to show that it sensibly diminishes with the lapse of time. Even when at its utmost height, affection contains within it the principle of its own decay. Indeed, there is nothing which remains forever in the same state of excellence, for virtue itself, upon attaining to a fullness, perishes in his own excess. What course of action we determine to take, ought to be taken at the moment of determination; for our determinations are apt to undergo alteration, and every person who intervenes, or is consulted, every trifling chance that occurs, helps to weaken their force or postpone their fulfilment. And, then, this feeling of duty, without the determination to perform it, enfeebles the moral nature, just as a sigh enfeebles the physical nature. But, to put the matter to a crucial test: you have heard that Hamlet has returned. How far are you willing to go, to show by your actions the genuineness of your protestations?

**Laertes:** I would murder him even in a sanctuary.

**King:** It is true that however sacred a place may be, it should not give refuge to one who has shed blood. The opportunity for vengeance ought to be seized wherever it occurs. Yet, my dear Laertes, I only ask you to follow these instructions. Confine yourself to your rooms. When Hamlet arrives, we shall tell him that you have returned from France. Some persons will also be incited to extol your skill, and to unduly exaggerate the praise which the Norman lavished upon you, the result being that a contest will be arranged between you, and money staked as to which of you will win. As Hamlet is very careless, besides being of a noble and unsuspicious nature, he will never think of examining the weapons. It will thus be a simple matter, or at any rate one requiring very little trickery on your part to select an unblunted rapier, and, with a treacherous thrust, to obtain satisfaction for your father's murder.

**Laertes:** I agree to your plan, only to make more sure of his death I intend to smear the end of my foil with a preparation I purchased from a quack, a preparation so deadly in its effects that, if a person be but pricked, however slightly, with an instrument dipped in it, his death is inevitable. However trifling the wound may seem, it is impossible to prepare a plaster from any of the herbs that grow upon this earth that will save his life. I'll smear the end of my foil with this liquid in order that the merest scratch may be attended with fatal results.

**King:** We had better give this matter additional consideration that we may take full advantage of any circumstance or opportunity which may occur to enable us to act out our parts successfully. For it would be more to our advantage not to attempt it at all than that our plans should miscarry, or our real intentions leak out owing to unskilful arrangements. It is my opinion, then, that we should hold some other scheme in reserve, lest our former one should fall to pieces on being put to the test. Stay now while I consider for a moment. Money will be staked with becoming seriousness upon your respective skill. Now I have hit upon it. During the progress of the contest, when you have become so heated and thirsty (in order to accomplish this end, see that the rounds are very furious) that Hamlet asks for wine, I shall hand him a cup containing a drink specially mixed for the occasion, the least taste of which will accomplish our purpose, even though your poisoned rapier may fail in its action. Hark! What is that sound I hear?

*[Enter queen.]*

What is the matter, my dear lady?

**Queen:** Our troubles succeed each other so rapidly that before we have finished with one, another occurs. Ophelia has perished in the water, Laertes.

**Laertes:** In the water? Whereabouts?

**Queen:** Overhanging a small rivulet there grows a willow, and the silvery gray of the underside of its leaves is clearly reflected in the pure water. To this spot came your sister carrying with her, wreaths quaintly fashioned out of buttercups, daisies, nettles and a kind of wild orchid, purple in color, which has received from our free-spoken herdsman a rather course name, but which is generally referred to by the chaste members of the opposite sex as dead men's fingers. Making her way along the sloping trunk and endeavoring to suspend her crown of flowers from one of its branches, a bough broke (one could almost have imagined it to have been moved by spite) and the poor girl dropped into the water beneath, carrying her flowers with her.

As her garments extended themselves upon the surface of the stream, she floated for some time like a sea maid, during which she sang portions of old songs as if she were quite insensible of her pitiable plight, or as if she were some being specially fitted by Providence to be at home in the water. She could not, however, remain for any length of time in this position, for her clothes, becoming saturated with water, dragged the dear creature to the bottom of the stream, and her tuneful song was hushed forever.

**Laertes:** Ah, me! Ophelia, then, has also perished.

**Queen:** Yes, perished in the stream.

**Laertes:** As you are already covered with water, my dear sister, I will do my best to restrain the moisture of my eyes. Still, it is a habit not easily shaken off; our natural inclinations get the better of us, however much we blush to own it. But after these few are shed, I shall have done with tears. Goodbye, your majesty. Words of burning indignation would even now burst forth from my lips were it not that this temporary weakness of mine extinguishes them.

**King:** We must go after him, Gertrude. It was as much as I could do before to soothe his indignation, but I shall not be surprised if this news makes him as furious as ever he was, so I think we had better go after him.

[*Exit.*]

# ACT V · SCENE 1

[*A churchyard.*]
[*Enter two clowns with shovels, etc.*]

**First Clown:** And do you mean to say that she is going to be buried by the Church, after intentionally taking her own life?

**Second Clown:** I do; so you had better complete your work without delay. The result of the inquest is that she may be thus interred.

**First Clown:** I do not know how they could return such a verdict unless they decided that she was justified in acting as she did.

**Second Clown:** Well, that is precisely what they did decide.

**First Clown:** Yes, the verdict can have been no other than that of justifiable homicide. This, in fact, is the crux of the matter. If I intentionally put an end to my life by throwing myself into the river, it may be fairly said that I have done something. Now every deed may be divided into three parts—achieving, accomplishing, and carrying out. Therefore, you see she must have known exactly what she was doing.

**Second Clown:** Listen to me, however, my dear knight of the shovel.

**First Clown:** No, let me finish first. Suppose, for instance, the river is here; just so: and the person yonder; just so: well, should the person walk to the river and throw himself in, he does it whether he wishes to do it or not; do you not see? But if the river should come and overwhelm him, then he cannot be said to have done it himself. It follows, therefore, that a person cannot be accused of curtailing the length of his own life if he did not kill himself.

**Second Clown:** Is that a sample of legal argumentation?

**First Clown:** Yes, indeed, it is, of the arguments you hear at a coroner's inquest.

**Second Clown:** I can tell you the real fact of the matter. If this lady had not been of noble birth, she would not have been favored by receiving this privilege.

**First Clown:** There is much truth in that remark, and I think it is a matter for regret that there should be more encouragement for people of high degree to commit suicide than for their other fellow-Christians. Well, I must go to work. No nobleman's pedigree is worth boasting of, in comparison with that of those men who, like myself, dig with the spade. They alone keep up the occupation of their first ancestor.

**Second Clown:** Was Adam a nobleman?

**First Clown:** He certainly had arms before anyone else had them.

**Second Clown:** But he bore no arms.

**First Clown:** You are surely not a Christian, or else you read your Bible without comprehending its meaning. Does it not say there that our first parent used the spade? If so, he must have had arms. Let me ask you something else, and if you cannot make a reasonable reply, give in that you are—

**Second Clown:** Come, come.

**First Clown:** Tell me who it is that constructs a more enduring dwelling than any other workman you can mention.

**Second Clown:** Well, I should say the man who builds a gallows, for that device may have a thousand successive occupants and still remain in use.

**First Clown:** An exceedingly good and clever answer! The gallows, indeed, has many tenants; in what way, however, does it manage to have so many? Why, by putting them away as soon as it receives them. Again, you had better not say that the gallows outlives the church, or it may have you for one of its tenants before long. Come, have another try.

**Second Clown:** Which workman constructs the most enduring dwelling?

**First Clown:** Yes, answer that question, and you may give over for today.

**Second Clown:** Well, at last I have it.

**First Clown:** Out with it, then.

**Second Clown:** No, I am afraid I cannot answer.

*[Enter Hamlet and Horatio at a distance.]*

**First Clown:** Do not trouble yourself any more by trying to think it out then. A stupid fellow like you will never find the answer, however hard you may try. But if someone else should propose the riddle, tell him the gravedigger. The dwellings he constructs endure as long as the world endures. Be off now, and bring me a flagon of something to drink from Yaughan.

*[He digs and sings.]*

*[Exit second clown.]*

I have a great dislike now for many things I was once very fond of; things which, as a young man, I considered very pleasant. But my time of life compels me to confess that they are no longer suitable for me.

**Hamlet:** That gravedigger is surely incapable of realizing the solemnity of his task or he would scarcely sing while at his work.

**Horatio:** He has been a gravedigger so long that it has become quite natural to him to take his occupation lightly.

**Hamlet:** That is always the case. Those who do least work with their hands have the most delicate touch.

**First Clown:** *[Sings.]* The years have flown swiftly and silently by, until at last Old Time has caught me in his firm embrace, and transported me into a state of weakness and senility, in which my vigorous youth seems almost a dream.

*[Throws up a skull.]*

**Hamlet:** That is all that remains of a head which at one time was endowed with the organs of speech. Notice how the rascal dashes it down with no more concern than if it were the skull of Cain, who was the first to take human life. I daresay it once adorned the shoulders of one who was a rare plotter and schemer in his time, one, maybe, who tried to outwit the Deity Himself. And now, even this stupid fellow has got the better of him.

**Horatio:** It is very probable, your lordship.

**Hamlet:** Again, it may have belonged to someone in the retinue of a monarch, to some smooth-tongued person, who delighted in the use of honeyed phrases; who could extol the steed of another in such pleasing terms, that the owner would be moved to present him with it. Is that not so?

**Horatio:** It is, your lordship.

**Hamlet:** Well, look at it now: it belongs to the worms; its jaws are gone; and a gravedigger batters it on the cranium with his shovel. This is, indeed, a startling change of fortune, if we only had the faculty of understanding it. Was so much pain and trouble expended on the rearing of these bones of ours, merely in order that someone might have a game of skittles with them? The very thought of it is torture to my own.

**First Clown:** *[Sings.]* What are the proper accompaniments of my time of life? An axe and a shovel, to prepare the grave destined to receive my corpse, carefully wrapped in its burial clothes.

[*Throws up another skull.*]

**Hamlet:** What, one more! Perhaps the head of someone well versed in the law. I wonder what has happened to the trivialities and nice distinctions; to the causes, leases, and legal artifices that once formed the chief part of his stock-in-trade. He even permits that impudent rogue to crack him across the pate with his filthy spade without threatening to have him charged with assault. Yet, I daresay he has, in his time, transferred huge estates by means of his acknowledgments, bonds, fines, testimonies, deeds and such like documents. Can he show no more than this from all his connection with the law? It is surely a poor return for all the documents he has assisted in drawing up, to have that clever head of his filled with rich soil. Surely his documents, doubly attested, entitle him to a more substantial share of what he has bought, than the mere parchment upon which the contracts were written. Even the title deeds by which the lands he possessed were transferred to his successor will hardly fit into the coffin, which is now all that their erstwhile owner can call his own. Is it not?

**Horatio:** That is his sole property now, your lordship.

**Hamlet:** Is it not true that the material of which these deeds are composed is prepared from the hides of sheep?

**Horatio:** Yes, your lordship, and from the hides of calves also.

**Hamlet:** It is fitting that it is so, for those who trust in such evidences of ownership are as foolish as the animals from which the material is prepared. I intend to question this knave. To whom does this tomb belong, my man?

**First Clown:** To me, your honor. [*Sings.*] A grave thus prepared in the earth is the fitting home for a person of my years.

**Hamlet:** You do well to say that, sir, for you are lying in it.

**First Clown:** Using a similar argument, it cannot belong to you, for you are lying out of it. Still, I affirm, that though I am not lying in it, the tomb belongs to me.

**Hamlet:** And I repeat that you are lying in it while you stand there and say that it is yours. A grave is not intended for the living, but for the departed. It follows, then, that you are not speaking the truth.

**First Clown:** Well, it is an untruth, your honor, that moves very rapidly; and it will shortly pass from me and attach itself to you.

**Hamlet:** Tell me the name of the man for whom you are preparing it.

**First Clown:** I am not preparing it for any man, your honor.

**Hamlet:** If not, let me know the lady's name.

**First Clown:** Nor am I preparing it for a lady.

**Hamlet:** Whose body then, is it intended to contain?

**First Clown:** The body of one who, in her lifetime was a lady, but she lives no longer. May she repose in peace!

**Hamlet:** This fellow is certainly a stickler for accuracy of speech. We had better be precise in our language, for if we use ambiguous words, we shall be ruined. By Jove, Horatio, for a long time now it has become evident to me that the people of this generation have grown so smart that the common folk are almost a match for the cleverest wits of the court. At least, they approach them very closely. For how many years have you followed this occupation?

**First Clown:** I can tell you the very day upon which my duties commenced. It was upon the occasion of the famous duel between our monarch and the late king of Norway.

**Hamlet:** How many years ago may that be?

**First Clown:** Do you mean to say you do not know? I did not think anyone was so stupid as not to know that. Why, the duel and the birth of Prince Hamlet occurred on the very same day. I mean the prince who has taken leave of his senses and has been banished to England in consequence.

**Hamlet:** Indeed, what induced them to choose England as his place of banishment?

**First Clown:** His insanity, of course. He may get better over there and be perfectly sane again but, even if he does not, it will make very little difference in that country.

**Hamlet:** In what way?

**First Clown:** Because nobody will notice it in England. The majority of the people there are lunatics.

**Hamlet:** What caused him to become insane?

**First Clown:** It is reported that the cause was a very singular one.

**Hamlet:** Singular, how so?

**First Clown:** In sooth, sir, he actually took leave of his senses.

**Hamlet:** But where was the provocation?

**First Clown:** In this very country. It is now thirty years ago since, as a mere lad, I became gravedigger here.

**Hamlet:** How many years must elapse before a corpse becomes thoroughly decomposed?

**First Clown:** Truth to tell, if decomposition has not already set in before we lay it in the earth, about eight years will be required. The body of a tanner, however, must be a year longer than this.

**Hamlet:** Why should his body be an exception to the rule?

**First Clown:** Well, his occupation, your honor, has almost turned his own skin into leather and made it waterproof. It is moisture, above all things, that hastens the decomposition of corpses. Look at this. It is twenty-three years since the owner of that head was laid to rest.

**Hamlet:** To whom did it belong?

**First Clown:** To a fool if ever there was one. Can you not guess to whom it belonged?

**Hamlet:** I cannot, indeed.

**First Clown:** Curses upon the knave for his mischievous pranks. Why, on one occasion he emptied the contents of a huge wine cup over me. This, your honor, was the head of Yorick, the fool of the Royal Household.

**Hamlet:** That skull?

**First Clown:** Yes, that one.

**Hamlet:** May I have it? [*Takes the skull.*] And so, this is all that is left of my old friend Yorick. He was my companion once, Horatio. What an endless fund of humor he possessed! What a splendid imagination! I remember I used to delight as a boy to ride upon his shoulders. And this thing, how loathsome it is to fancy, how sick I feel at the thought that this was the face I loved to fondle and caress! What have you done with those taunts, those pranks, those melodies, and those sparkling witticisms that used to convulse all who heard them? Cannot you utter a single one now even to ridicule the hideous look upon your face? Go, take this to the boudoir of her ladyship, and let her know that no matter how much care she may bestow upon the beautification of her complexion, this will one day be the appearance of her features. Make her see the humor of that. Say, Horatio, enlighten me upon this point.

**Horatio:** What point, your lordship?

**Hamlet:** Do you suppose that the great king of Macedon appeared thus after burial?

**Horatio:** I certainly do.

**Hamlet:** And had a similar odor? Ugh!

*[Puts down the skull.]*

**Horatio:** Undoubtedly, your lordship.

**Hamlet:** Truly, Horatio, our remains may have to serve ignoble ends. It is not difficult for instance to follow, in fancy, the remains of even so mighty a man as the king we have just mentioned until they are discovered at length damning up the hole in a cask.

**Horatio:** I should think that to do so would require much ingenious and fanciful reasoning.

**Hamlet:** Not at all, in very truth. I can trace them thus far, not only without much ingenuity, but with much probability. Listen now. When Alexander's body was laid in the tomb, it was gradually transformed into the earth from which it originally sprang. What is there to prevent that earth, more than any other, from being converted into the substance which is used for closing up bungholes? Yes, it is quite possible for the dust of the great emperor Julius, after being changed into loam, to be used for the purpose of closing up a crack to keep out the draft. It is a solemn thought that the very substance which held the whole earth in dread should, in the end, have to repair a wall and make it impervious to the sudden gusts of wintry wind. Let us be silent, however, and withdraw. I see that his majesty is approaching.

*[Enter priests, etc., in procession; the corpse of Ophelia; Laertes and mourners following; king, queen and their trains, etc.]*

My mother and all the nobles of the court! I wonder whose funeral they attend, that is stripped of so many of its usual ceremonies. By this I perceive that the person who is to be buried laid violent hands upon herself. She must have been of high rank too. Let us screen ourselves from observation and notice what happens.

*[Retiring with Horatio.]*

**Laertes:** Must there be no other rites than these?

**Hamlet:** Laertes is speaking, a young man of gentle birth.

Notice.

**Laertes:** Must there be no other rites than these?

**First Priest:** We have said as much of the burial service as we have authority for doing. It is not clear whether she willfully took her life or not, and were it not that his majesty has overruled the course which the Church prescribes on such occasions, we should have laid her to rest in unconsecrated ground, there to remain until the Judgment Day. Instead of the prayers of compassionate souls, stones and fragments of pottery would have been showered upon her. In spite of this, she has been permitted to have her maiden garlands, to have flowers scattered over her casket, and to be accompanied to her last resting place by the tolling of a funeral bell.

**Laertes:** And will you grant her nothing further?

**First Priest:** Nothing. To chant a mass for the repose of her soul, as we do for the souls of those who have passed calmly and quietly from this life, would be a mere violation of the holy office of burial.

**Laertes:** Let her rest beneath the soil, and God grant that the ashes of her comely and unsullied body may bring forth sweet spring flowers! Servant of the Church though you are, your surly uncharitableness assures me that you will one day in torment crave the soothing touch of her angelic hand.

**Hamlet:** Heavens, it is his lovely sister, Ophelia!

**Queen:** Lovely flowers for a lovely maid: good-bye! [*Scattering flowers.*] I hoped, dear one, to have the pleasure of using these flowers to adorn thy nuptial chamber, instead of scattering them upon thy tomb.

**Laertes:** May the threefold grief inflicted upon me by the accursed wretch who maliciously destroyed thy keen intelligence, recoil upon him with tenfold force! Do not fill in the grave yet for a few moments, but allow me to give my sister a final embrace.

[*Leaps into the grave.*]

Throw the earth upon us both now, and stay not your hands until upon this level surface you have raised a mound, higher than the weather-worn summit of Pelion, or even the lofty Olympus, the top of which almost touches the azure vault of heaven.

**Hamlet:** [*Advancing.*] Who can this be, who lays such mighty stress upon his woe, who proclaims his grief in words which charm the very planets, and make them halt in their courses, struck with astonishment? I am Hamlet, Prince of Denmark.

[*Leaps into the grave.*]

**Laertes:** Perdition seize thee!

[*Grappling with him.*]

**Hamlet:** That is scarcely a charitable entreaty. Let me urge you, sir, not to grasp me so fiercely. It is not my nature to be passionate and headstrong. Still, a certain quality lurks within me, which, if you are prudent, you will be afraid of. Let me go then.

**King:** Drag them apart.

**Queen:** My son, my son!

**All:** Sirs.

**Horatio:** My gracious lordship, do not strive with him.

[*The attendants part them, and they come out of the grave.*]

**Hamlet:** I intend to contend with him upon this subject as long as I retain sufficient vitality to open and shut my eyes.

**Queen:** Upon what subject, my dear Hamlet?

**Hamlet:** The subject of his regard for his sister. The sum total of the affection of countless brothers could not nearly equal mine. Tell me what acts you are willing to perform for her sake.

**King:** Do not heed his ravings, Laertes.

**Queen:** And for mercy's sake, do not attempt to touch him.

**Hamlet:** Come now, let me hear what you are willing to do. Do you tell me that you will shed oceans of tears, engage in dangerous conflicts, abstain from all food, swallow the bitterest of drafts and chew the toughest of hides? Well, so will I. Did you make up your mind to utter plaintive moans, and to endeavor to shame me with extravagant protestations of affection? If you are willing to be interred alive with her, I am too. And, as for your ranting talk about mountains, they may cast fields of earth upon us, if they like, so that the summit of the mound will touch the scorching sun itself, causing Ossa to appear like a mere skin eruption in comparison with it. Moreover, if you are going to rage and brag, I can be your equal even at that.

**Queen:** Heed not this outburst, which is only one of his sudden attacks of insanity. It will hold him in its power for a time, but passing soon, he will hang his head, mute and ashamed, and be as difficult to provoke as a hen pigeon, whose yellow pair of fluffy nestlings are newly hatched.

**Hamlet:** Hearken to me, Laertes. How is it that you persist in rejecting my friendly advances? I have always had a liking for you. Still it is no use complaining. Not even the strongest of men can prevent matters from taking their appointed course. The cat will squeal, and the dog have his good time, whatever may be done to prevent them.

*[Exit.]*

**King:** My dear Horatio, let me beseech you to attend him, so that he may meet with no harm.

*[Exit Horatio.]*

*[To Laertes.]* Let the conversation we had together yesterday assist you in putting up with him for a while. We will take steps to put our plan into immediate operation. My dear wife, see that someone is appointed to look after Hamlet. The memory of this departed one shall be perpetuated by the sacrifice of a life. Soon now shall we be free from this care and anxiety, and until that time arrives, let us see that we act with calmness and discretion.

*[Exit.]*

## ACT V · SCENE 2

*[A hall in the castle.]*
*[Enter Hamlet and Horatio.]*

**Hamlet:** Well, Horatio, enough of that matter. Let me now tell you about the other. I suppose you recollect the condition of affairs.

**Horatio:** Of course I do, your lordship.

**Hamlet:** Well, within me a species of conflict was raging, which drove slumber from my eyelids. I fancied my plight would not bear comparison even with that of rebellious sailors in irons. I followed a sudden impulse, and am thankful that I did. Such risks sometimes work out, as in this case, and make one believe in a guiding Providence.

**Horatio:** I quite agree with you in that.

**Hamlet:** Throwing my sailor's robe loosely round me, without putting my arms through the sleeves, I left my room and felt my way in the gloom, to the place where the dispatches were kept. Having succeeded in laying my hands upon them, I at length returned with them to my cabin once more, and there I was sufficiently daring, and in my apprehension sufficiently dishonorable too, to open the communication which they had guarded with such great care. You will scarcely believe that a king could possibly be guilty of such villainy when I tell you that it contained a peremptory order, garnished with different excuses justifying such a course, excuses which concerned the welfare of the king of England as well as of Denmark, and suggested that terrible dangers threatened if I continued to live, that as soon as it had been read over, without allowing any moments of relaxation, without even waiting until the axe should be sharpened, I was to be beheaded.

**Horatio:** Can it indeed be true?

**Hamlet:** Well, let me give you the document itself, which you may peruse when opportunity offers. Do you wish, however, to know what steps I took next?

**Horatio:** I entreat you to tell me.

**Hamlet:** Seeing then that I was completely entangled in the coils of their wicked schemes, before I had formed any real plan of action, my mind was actively engaged in carrying it out. I took my pen, thought out a second dispatch, and executed the same in a good legible hand. At one time I was of the same opinion as our statesmen that plain legible handwriting is a mark of low birth, and I took infinite pains to unlearn that accomplishment. I am glad, however, that I was unsuccessful, for it was of the utmost value to me in this crisis. Would you like me to tell you the purport of my letter?

**Horatio:** Certainly, your highness.

**Hamlet:** It was a solemn charge from our sovereign, calling upon his loyal subject monarch, the English king, provided that he wished their regard for each other to thrive luxuriantly, provided that he wished his land to continue to enjoy the blessings of peace and plenty, and the two nations to be separated as little as possible in their regard for each other, and various other weighty provisions of a similar nature, to execute the persons entrusted with this dispatch as soon as he had read it, without staying even a moment to consider, or allowing them time for confession and absolution.

**Horatio:** But what about the impression on the dispatch?

**Hamlet:** Well, in that respect, too, Providence seemed to have directed matters. I carried in my purse a ring bearing my father's privy seal, an exact counterpart of the one upon the original commission. I folded the counterfeit document in exact imitation of the real one, affixed the king's signature to it, sealed it up and laid it just where I had found the other, so that no one could possibly guess it had been tampered with. On the following day, we had our adventure with the pirate, and I have already acquainted you with the remainder of my adventures.

**Horatio:** Then your two friends are sailing toward their doom?

**Hamlet:** What of that? They voluntarily courted this duty of spying upon me, and must take the consequences. Their death does not cause me any uneasiness. It is the natural result of meddling in matters which were not their business. Persons of inferior character who interpose themselves between the swords of two powerful opponents, thrusting at each other with fierceness and anger, must be prepared to take all risks.

**Horatio:** This person is certainly not fit to be our sovereign.

**Hamlet:** Is it not your opinion that it is incumbent upon me, that it is perfectly justifiable for me, to obtain satisfaction personally from this fellow, who poisoned my father and brought reproach upon my mother, thrust himself between me and my expectation of being chosen king, and endeavored, and so cunningly too, to achieve my death? Would it not be a crime worthy of eternal destruction to allow this blight upon humanity to continue his wicked career?

**Horatio:** News will soon reach the king from England acquainting him with the result of the commission he sent.

**Hamlet:** Yes, he will know presently, but then I have the interval in which to act, and to take a man's life is but the work of a moment. Nevertheless, Horatio, I feel grieved at my discourteous behaviour toward Laertes, for his grievance is almost exactly the counterpart of my own. I will do my best to appease him, though I must confess, his ostentatious display of feeling thoroughly roused my indignation.

**Horatio:** Be quiet, someone is approaching.

[*Enter Osric.*]

**Osric:** My lord, your country is really pleased to behold you once again.

**Hamlet:** Accept my gratitude, sir, for your undeserved compliment. Are you acquainted with this dandy?

**Horatio:** I am not, your lordship.

**Hamlet:** You are fortunate in that respect then, for it is anything but an honor to be acquainted with him. His estate is large and very productive, so of course he sits at the king's table, as any person, however bestial, is allowed to do, provided only that he has plenty of property. He is a boor, but, as I remarked, is tolerated on account of his wide acres.

**Osric:** If your gracious lordship has a few moments to spare, I have a message to you from his royal highness the king.

**Hamlet:** I am always ready to listen to any communication from such a source. But, my lord, you will please me by making your hat perform its intended service and wearing it.

**Osric:** You are exceedingly kind, my lord, but I carry it on account of the excessive heat.

**Hamlet:** You are mistaken, I think. It blows from the north, so it is anything but hot.

**Osric:** To tell the truth, your lordship, it is rather chilly.

**Hamlet:** And still I fancy it is exceedingly close and oppressive, else my temperament—

**Osric:** Most assuredly, your lordship, somehow or other, I do not know how to explain it, it is oppressive. But, your lordship, I am commissioned by our sovereign to acquaint you with the fact that he has staked a large sum of money upon your skill. My lord, it is for this reason that—

**Hamlet:** Let me urge you to bear in mind—

[*Hamlet makes him put on his hat.*]

**Osric:** My discourtesy was unintentional, your gracious lordship. It was for my own comfort that I removed it, really. My lord, a nobleman has recently arrived at the palace, who is, I assure you, a perfect courtier. He is distinguished from the rest of his fellows by many splendid qualities. His manners are irreproachable and he is brilliant in the extreme. In fact, to do justice to his merits, he is the very pattern of all that a gentleman should be, and possesses the sum total of all the qualities that one ought to possess.

**Hamlet:** My lord, your description of him does him no injustice, although I am aware that to attempt to catalogue his many excellences would overtask and confuse the mental faculties, and still lag lamentably behind his deserts. Indeed, to praise him with the strictest regard for truth he is a person of so many perfections, and his natural gifts would be so difficult to find elsewhere combined in the same person, that with a due regard for fact, no one but himself could be his equal, and those who attempt to imitate him are, at best, merely his shadow.

**Osric:** You describe him, your highness, as if you could not possibly be mistaken with regard to him.

**Hamlet:** What is the meaning of it all, sir? What is the use of attempting to describe such a paragon in our feeble language?

**Osric:** I beg your pardon.

**Horatio:** What, cannot you comprehend your own jargon when spoken by another? Use your wits, sir, and you will certainly succeed.

**Hamlet:** Why has Laertes' name been introduced into the conversation?

**Osric:** His name?

**Horatio:** His treasury of beautiful language is already exhausted. All his fine words have flown.

**Hamlet:** Yes, his name.

**Osric:** I am sure you cannot be without knowledge—

**Hamlet:** I wish, indeed, that you were, sir, and still, in truth, even if you were, it would not be a very great commendation. Go on, my lord.

**Osric:** You are not without knowledge of Laertes' skill—

**Hamlet:** I am afraid to acknowledge so much, lest I should pretend to be his equal; for a man can know only so much of another as he knows of himself.

**Osric:** I refer, my lord, to his skill in arms. In the estimation of the majority of people, no one can equal him in merit.

**Hamlet:** In what particular branch of arms does he specially excel?

**Osric:** In the use of the foil and dagger.

**Hamlet:** I said "branch," not "branches." But never mind; go on.

**Osric:** His majesty, my lord, has staked six fine North African steeds, and Laertes, I am given to understand, has pledged against them six swords and daggers of French manufacture, together with all their proper accompaniments, such as the belts, the small straps by which they are attached to the belts, and the like. With regard to the carriages, half of them are really of a very artistic character, quite in keeping with the handles. They are very finely worked indeed, and most tasteful in design.

**Hamlet:** Whatever do you mean by carriages?

**Horatio:** I was sure that some comment would be necessary before you were finished.

**Osric:** I mean, my lord, the small straps alluded to above.

**Hamlet:** The expression would be a more suitable one if we were in the habit of suspending big guns from our belts. Till we do that, I prefer to hear them called by their proper name. Proceed, however: six fine North African steeds against the same number of rapiers of French manufacture, together with all that appertains to them, including three carriages, very tasteful in design. The stakes are thoroughly representative of the two nationalities. Why, to use your own expression, have these been pledged?

**Osric:** His majesty, my lord, has wagered that out of twelve bouts between Laertes and yourself, the former shall not thrust you three times more than you thrust him. The wager is twelve against nine, and the match will take place at once, provided that your highness will condescend to respond.

**Hamlet:** But suppose I respond in the negative?

**Osric:** By "respond," your highness, I wish to signify "accept the challenge to fence."

**Hamlet:** As this is the part of the day I usually devote to exercise, I shall be walking about here for some time, and if Laertes wishes to meet me, and his majesty has not changed his mind, I shall do my best to gain the victory for him. Should I fail, disgrace, and the extra thrusts, will be my only portion.

**Osric:** Am I to report that such is your decision?

**Hamlet:** This is the substance of it. You may clothe it in whatever affected language you please.

**Osric:** My services are ever at your highness' command.

**Hamlet:** Allow me to return the compliment. [*Exit Osric.*] He has every reason for personally offering his services, for I am sure that no one else would recommend them.

**Horatio:** That fellow is as forward and presumptuous as a young gull.

**Hamlet:** He is a born courtier. I have no doubt that before using his mother's breast, he apologized to it for the liberty he was about to take. He, along with numerous others with whom I am acquainted, and who are popular favorites in these degenerate days, has merely caught the prevailing note of the times, and its exterior politeness of address. With this frothy assemblage of accomplishments, these young gentlemen air their foolish and fantastic notions. And yet, one has merely to test them by blowing, and they burst like bubbles.

*[Enter a lord.]*

**Lord:** Your lordship, young Osric, whom the king entrusted with a message for you, has informed his majesty that you are waiting for him here. His majesty desires you to inform him whether you will be pleased to encounter Laertes at once, or whether you would rather postpone the meeting till some future date.

**Hamlet:** I adhere to my former decision, and shall play whenever his majesty desires me to do so. Should he consider this a suitable time, I am quite prepared. In fact I will fight at once, or at any other time he chooses, if only I am in as good form as I am at present.

**Lord:** Their majesties and followers will be here immediately.

**Hamlet:** They have chosen the right moment.

**Lord:** It is her majesty's wish that you should say a few conciliatory words to your opponent before the match begins.

**Hamlet:** The advice is good, and I shall follow it.

*[Exit lord.]*

**Horatio:** I am afraid you will not win in this contest, your lordship.

**Hamlet:** I rather fancy I shall. During his stay abroad I have practised daily, and besides, look at the advantage he has given me. Yet, Horatio, you can have no idea what a sinking feeling I have within me. But what of that?

**Horatio:** On the other hand, your lordship—

**Hamlet:** It is nothing but a silly feeling; a sort of misgiving that ought never, under any circumstances, to trouble a man.

**Horatio:** If you have any misgivings I advise you to give heed to them. Let me go to them, before they come, and tell them that you do not feel in good condition for the contest.

**Hamlet:** Not on any account. I entirely disregard presentiments. Not even the smallest of creatures can die before its appointed time. If this be mine, I cannot postpone it; if mine be not in the future, it must be in the present; and if it be not in the present, its arrival is inevitable. To be prepared, that is everything. As no one has a firm hold of any portion of that which he must relinquish at his death, what matters how soon he dies? Allow matters, then, to take their course.

*[Enter king, queen, Laertes and lords; Osric and other attendants, with foils and gauntlets, a table and cups of wine upon it.]*

**King:** Hamlet, my son, let me make peace between you by uniting your hands.

*[The king puts Laertes' hand into Hamlet's.]*

**Hamlet:** Grant me forgiveness, Laertes. I acknowledge that you have just cause of complaint against me. Yet forgive me, as a person of your rank should do. All in this company are aware, and I am sure that you, too, cannot be ignorant of the malady which afflicts me. Every word or deed of mine by which I may have rudely irritated your natural or honorable instincts, or which may have earned your disapproval, I solemnly declare was spoken or done under the influence of that malady. If, sir, I have ever injured you in any way, be assured it was not my real self that did it. If the part of me which constitutes my real personality be absent from myself, and the remainder do you an injury, surely I cannot be accused of doing it. I entirely disown such conduct. In that case who can be the guilty one? Why, my insanity. Grant me this, then, and I, too, am one of those who have been injured. I am in the pitiable condition of having been wronged by my own insanity. Laertes, as I have, before the whole company present, repudiated the charge of having inflicted an intentional injury upon you, allow your natural kindliness of disposition to believe me when I say that I acted like a boy who, thoughtlessly aiming his darts over the roof of his dwelling, has wounded someone very dear to him on the other side.

**Laertes:** So far as my natural feelings are concerned, you have quite made amends by your apology. And yet I confess that these feelings ought strongly to urge me to seek vengeance. Whether or not, however, your apology satisfies the demands of the code of chivalry, I decline to say, and I refuse to entertain any thought of renewing our friendship until some, who by their age and experience are recognized as authorities in such matters, have given an opinion and cited a case in point to show that I am justified in being reconciled to you, and that I may be so without any injury to my reputation. Pending such a decision, however, I accept your friendly advances as what they profess to be, and will in no way injure them by doubting their genuineness.

**Hamlet:** I receive your reply with gladness, and will engage in this combat as unreservedly as if we were children of the same parents. Now, sir, bring hither the weapons.

**Laertes:** Hand me a foil, too.

**Hamlet:** My want of skill, Laertes, will serve as a perfect foil to your dexterity, making it stand out in brilliant relief, like a shining planet against the inky background of the heavens.

**Laertes:** Do not be sarcastic, I pray you.

**Hamlet:** I am not in the least sarcastic, I swear it.

**King:** Well, Osric, let them have the weapons. I suppose, Hamlet, you have been told what the stakes are?

**Hamlet:** I have, your highness, and I think I am so much the inferior of Laertes that the difference is still in his favor.

**King:** I do not share your opinion. I know your respective skill, but since Laertes is the superior, I have made him concede you points.

**Laertes:** There is too much weight in this foil for me. Hand me another.

**Hamlet:** Mine suits me splendidly. I suppose they are all as long as each other.

*[They prepare to play.]*

**Osric:** Certainly, your lordship.

**King:** Fill the large drinking cups with wine and place them before me, and should our cousin be successful in either of the first two encounters, or pay him off by making a hit in the third, give orders for a simultaneous discharge of artillery from every tower. His majesty shall honor a toast wishing Hamlet sufficient endurance to last out the combat, and shall place in the goblet a fine pearl of greater value than the one set in the diadem, which has graced the brows of the four preceding kings of our land. Place the goblets near me and see that the roll of the drum proclaims to the trumpeter, that the trumpeter announces to the gunner on the battlements, that the clash of artillery proclaims to the skies, and the skies re-echo to earth again, that his majesty proposes a toast to Hamlet's success. Now, gentlemen, commence; and umpires, see that you observe their movements closely.

**Hamlet:** I am ready, Laertes.

**Laertes:** And I, your lordship.

[*They play.*]

**Hamlet:** One for me.

**Laertes:** Not at all.

**Hamlet:** What say the umpires?

**Osric:** Without doubt a thrust, and an obvious one too.

**Laertes:** Let us commence once more then.

**King:** Hold; hand me the goblet. Hamlet, I place this pearl here for you and pledge your success.

[*Trumpets sound, and cannon shot off within.*]
Pass it to him.

**Hamlet:** Let it stand a moment until we finish this encounter. Commence. [*They play.*] A point for me again. Do you not think so?

**Laertes:** I admit you touched me, only slightly, however.

**King:** Hamlet is sure to be victorious now.

**Queen:** He is out of training. Hamlet, my son, wipe your forehead with this handkerchief, and I will drink to your success.

**Hamlet:** Thank you, mother.

**King:** My dear, do not touch the cup. It is for Hamlet.

**Queen:** Excuse me, your lordship, with your kind permission, I will.

**King:** [*Aside.*] It is the wine I have drugged. I cannot prevent her now.

**Hamlet:** It would be dangerous to drink at present. In a few moments I will.

**Queen:** Allow me, then, to wipe the moisture from your brows.

**Laertes:** I shall strike him in this encounter, your majesty.

**King:** I am afraid you will not.

**Laertes:** [*Aside.*] Still it cuts me to the heart to be so treacherous.

**Hamlet:** Well, Laertes, are you ready to try again? You are trifling with me. Come, now, thrust with all your might, for I am beginning to suspect you are treating me as if I were a mere child.

**Laertes:** Do you think so? Well, commence.

**Osric:** Neither of you has made a hit.

**Laertes:** I swear I will hit him this time.

> [*Laertes wounds Hamlet; then, in scuffling they change rapiers, and Hamlet wounds Laertes.*]

**King:** Drag them away from each other. Their blood is up, and they fight in real earnest.

**Hamlet:** No, let us have another bout.

> [*The queen falls.*]

**Osric:** I say, attend to her majesty, she is ill.

**Horatio:** Both the combatants are wounded. How can you account for this, your lordship?

**Osric:** How do you account for it, Laertes?

**Laertes:** Like a decoy duck, Osric, caught in its own trap. I have deservedly been slain in consequence of my own treachery.

**Hamlet:** What ails the queen?

**King:** The sight of blood has caused her to faint.

**Queen:** Not at all, it is the wine I tasted, the wine—Hamlet, my son, there's death in that cup, death.

> [*Dies.*]

**Hamlet:** Some traitor is amongst us. I say, there, close all entrances, and permit no one to leave until we have discovered the author of this villainy.

**Laertes:** He is close by you, Hamlet. You, too, my friend, are done for; nowhere on this earth can an antidote be found to cure you. You cannot possibly live for thirty minutes longer. The dastardly outrage was performed with the unblunted and poisoned end of the foil you now hold in your hand. I also have fallen a victim to my own treacherous plot, and will rise no more from the spot upon which I have fallen. The queen has died of poison, but I have no power to say more, except that the king, your uncle, is the culprit.

**Hamlet:** So this is not only unblunted, but poisoned as well.

Then let the poison accomplish its purpose.

*[Stabs the king.]*

**All:** Ho! Treachery is afoot.

**King:** Help me, loyal subjects, I am merely wounded as yet.

**Hamlet:** Here, you licentious assassin, you cursed villain, take this and swallow it. Is that where you put the pearl? Go after the queen.

*[King dies.]*

**Laertes:** It is no more than he deserves. The poisonous draft was prepared by himself, specially for you. Let us be completely reconciled to each other before I die, Hamlet. May you never be called upon to answer for my own and my parent's death. May I never be called upon to answer for yours!

*[Dies.]*

**Hamlet:** I pray God to absolve you from all blame in the matter. I shall be with you soon. Horatio, I am done for. Good-bye, unhappy mother. Those of you who stand around with shaking limbs and ashen faces, silent spectators of these calamities, would, if I had time, hear strange tales from my lips. But I must forbear, for this cruel officer, death, will accept neither denial nor delay when once he has laid hands upon his victim. Horatio, though I depart, you still remain to give a true account of the reason why I acted as I did, to those who blame my conduct.

**Horatio:** Do not suppose for one moment that I could do such a thing. My nature resembles that of the Romans of old, rather than that of a Dane, and I prefer to take the remainder of the poison rather than outlive my friend.

**Hamlet:** If you have any manhood in you, refrain from such a course. Hand the poison to me, at once. At all hazards I must have it. Horatio, my kind friend, think what a sullied reputation will be mine unless you survive me to make known the true circumstances which compelled me to act as I did. Prove now the sincerity of the love you have professed for me by postponing for a time your departure to the realms of bliss, and deigning to endure the troubles of this mortal life in order that you may give a true account of my wrongs. *[Trumpets far off, and shots within.]* What martial sounds are these I hear?

**Osric:** The youthful Prince of Norway, returning victorious from his expedition against the Poles, is saluting the

English envoys with a discharge of artillery.

**Hamlet:** Horatio, I cannot live a moment longer, not even to learn the tidings which they bring. This powerful drug has completely conquered my vitality. Nevertheless, I am quite sure that the choice of a successor to the throne will fall upon Fortinbras. Let him know that with my last breath I supported his claim. Acquaint him also with every event, great and small, which induced me to act as I have acted. Death now closes my utterance.

[*Dies.*]

**Horatio:** A truly generous spirit is here forever broken. Farewell, beloved prince, and may the heavenly choir accompany thy soul as it speeds to its eternal abode! What has induced the martial music to come in this direction?

[*Music within.*]
[*Enter Fortinbras and the English ambassadors, with drums, colors and attendants.*]

**Fortinbras:** Is the spectacle here, which I am asked to behold?

**Horatio:** What spectacle, sir? If it be one as strange as it is mournful, you need look no farther.

**Fortinbras:** This heap of slain proclaims an indiscriminate slaughter. Surely the arrogant deity who numbers our days has some great banquet in preparation in his everlasting halls, else he would not, with one blow, have shed so much royal blood.

**First Ambassador:** It is indeed a mournful spectacle, and the news we bring from England will never reach the person for whom it was intended. He who ought to have granted us an opportunity of informing him that his instructions have been obeyed, and that the two envoys were duly executed, is now beyond the reach of all news. To whom shall we now look for an expression of gratitude for the trouble we have taken?

**Horatio:** It would have been useless to have looked to him, even if he were alive and able to thank you. No instructions for their execution ever proceeded from him.

Seeing, however, that you have both come upon the scene at the very moment of all this bloodshed, one from across the seas and the other from his expedition to Poland, command your attendants to expose these corpses to the public gaze upon an elevated platform, while I make known to the people, who as yet remain in ignorance, the cause of these events. My story will be a strange one, dealing as it does with sensual, murderous and inhuman deeds, with mistaken suppositions that caused unintentional death, with other fatalities, the result of the circumstances in which the perpetrator was placed by the crafty instigations of others, and finally, with schemes clumsily carried out, recoiling and bringing destruction upon the heads of those who conceived them. The whole of the foregoing I am able to narrate with absolute accuracy.

**Fortinbras:** We will make immediate preparations to listen to your account, and will see that your hearers include all those who hold high rank in this country. As for myself, in deepest grief, I proceed to take advantage of the opportunity which this singular combination of circumstances has placed in my way. I have some just claims to the crown of this land which are still remembered, and this opportunity urges me to assert them.

**Horatio:** I shall deal with that matter too in my recital, and you will find your claims supported by one whose recommendation will have much influence with many besides. See, however, that my instructions are carried out without delay, for these events have greatly excited the populace, and no one can tell in such cases what other misfortunes may occur, either by intention or by accident.

**Fortinbras:** Order four of the officers to support the bier upon which Hamlet is to be carried to the platform, seeing that, if circumstances had allowed, it is probable that he would have shown himself worthy of his kingly birth. Also, in respect of his memory, let a solemn march be played, and the cannon boom loudly over his body. Remove the fallen: the spectacle of so many slain, however suitable to a battle field, is entirely unsuitable to a place like this. Away, command the firing party to fulfil their duty.

> [*A solemn march. Exit, bearing off the dead bodies, after which a peal of cannons is shot off.*]

# NOTES